Fractal Design
Painter

DAWN ERDOS
and JANEY P. BRAND

MIS: PRESS

A Subsidiary of
Henry Holt and Co., Inc.

First Edition—1995

ISBN 1-55828-416-8

MIS:Press books are available at special discounts for bulk purchases for sales promotions, premiums, fund-raising, or educational use. Special editions or book excerpts can also be created to specification.

For details contact: Special Sales Director
MIS:Press
a subsidiary of Henry Holt and Company, Inc.
115 West 18th Street
New York, New York 10011

Book Design: Dawn Erdos
Cover Art: Kerry Gavin
Development Editor: Debra Williams Cauley
Production Editor: Patricia Wallenburg and Maya Riddick
Copy Editor: Shari Chappell
Index and Glossary: Janey P. Brand

DEDICATION

To Michael Erdos

who introduced us to the worlds of fine and commercial arts while we were still young and impressionable, and provided us with the foundation we needed to get where we are today.

ACKNOWLEDGMENTS

We would like to thank the many people who helped make this book possible:

Steve Guttman, Mark Zimmer, Daryl Wise, John Derry, Laurie Hemnes, Annette Hart and the Tech Support staff at Fractal Design Corporation for their valuable input and support.

Debra Williams Cauley, Development Editor, Cary Sullivan, Managing Editor, Shari Chappell, Copy Editor, Patricia Wallenburg and Maya Riddick, Production Editors, and Joe McPartland, Anne Alessi, and Eileen Mullin for all of their help in producing this book.

Dennis Orlando, Gary Clark, Kerry Gavin, and Richard Noble, as well as the many other talented artists in this book, for letting us pick their brains.

Meher, for leaving the country so I could get some work done.

Wahid Shiloh of Crystal Clear Computing in Sedona, Arizona, for incredible computer service and technical support during this project. His time and efforts are much appreciated.

CONTENTS

CONTENTS

CHAPTER 5: COLOR 57

CONTENTS

CONTENTS

CONTENTS

APPENDIX A: EXTENSIONS AND THIRD-PARTY SOFTWARE 195

PREFACE

Hi! I'm Mark Zimmer, the original and still primary author of Painter. When I was little I was an incessant artist. I worked in pencil, ballpoint pen, and fine-point felt marker, often in full color. By the time I was 18, I was drawing portraits and sketching landscapes. These early excursions into art and design were absolutely essential first steps on the path to Painter. But first, technology had to catch up.

I have long considered tablets and paint programs to be very interesting. In 1975 I started working at Calma, a computer-aided design company in Silicon Valley, where I met Tom Hedges (another author of Painter). There we were introduced to digitizing tables (which were as big as battleships then) made by CalComp. In 1983, at Tricad, I worked with a digitizing tablet, the Summagraphics Bit Pad One, and built my first 8-bit paint system as a way to retouch images created in a 3-D rendering environment I had written. In 1985, I started working on PatEdit, a program for latchhook rug design and pattern editing. That's when I first hit on the idea of simulating charcoal on a computer. Back then, there were only mice to draw with on the desktop. Wacom's cordless pressure-sensitive tablets were introduced for the desktop two years later, and it was only then that the concept of a natural-media paint program became feasible. By the way, PatEdit became GrayPaint, which finally became ImageStudio in 1987. By then Tom Hedges and I had formed Fractal Software. To Tom's credit, he saw the advent of scanners to be a primary reason to develop image processing software. So Tom and I developed ImageStudio and then ColorStudio for Letraset, and we were plunged fully into the world of image processing, color separation, visual effects, and incidentally, pressure support for our paint brushes.

But it wasn't until 1990 that I began work on Painter. With all of this image processing work, I began to feel that I had lost the focus of my original work: to make the computer a valid medium for artists. I had been working on a model for the interaction between pencil and paper since 1987, so I began to implement some of that research using a pressure-sensitive tablet and a Mac II at home. This experimentation became Painter. Finally, in 1991, we formed Fractal Design Corporation to market Painter.

So, I am especially pleased to see a book on our product. This book is beautifully illustrated and features sections on artists who work with Painter to create works of wonder. As I read over the proofs for this book, I have concluded that these pages should be required reading for any serious artist who wants to use the computer as a medium.

Mark Zimmer

President and Co-Founder

Fractal Design Corp.

Section I

Getting Started in Your Digital Studio

CHAPTER 1

INTRODUCTION

Welcome to Fractal Design Painter! With Painter you'll be able to work with all of the traditional art tools you're used to, as well as many new digital features. In addition to pen, pencil, chalk, pastels, oil paint, water colors, and masks, you now have access to powerful image-editing options that let you work with scanned photographs or illustrations, add light sources, adjust contrast, change density, sharpen images, create marbled effects, rotate, distort, and many other digital options. Painter also provides you with choices for surface textures, including different types of water color paper, canvas, and Bainbridge board.

There are many advantages to working in Painter's electronic studio: You never run out of paint or canvases. You don't have to worry about destroying your brushes if you don't clean them properly. You don't have to worry about the limits of your studio space. And you don't have to inhale toxic chemicals. You have a palette of 16 million colors—there aren't many traditional artists who have a palette like that! You can work dry media over wet media, for example, pastels over oil paint, and other unusual combinations of media can be used in new ways. You can literally apply a medium to *thousands* of tex-

tures, and you can even select individual areas in a painting to emphasize, such as the dimples on an orange.

In an electronic studio you also have the ability to try a vast array of effects on a painting without ever changing the original. The tools available in Painter allow you to explore other options without ever damaging a painting—you can try something different without destroying the original work!

Painter also enables you to view detail and composition simply by clicking your mouse. You can zoom into the most minute detail, then zoom all the way back to view it as if you were 10 feet away.

We interviewed a lot of artists while creating this book. We kept hearing phrases such as "it's like magic" over and over again. As you'll read in Section II, many artists feel Painter has not only changed the way they work, but the attitude and enthusiasm with which they do that work.

TECHNICAL CONSIDERATIONS

One of the features of Painter that is often highly praised is its natural, intuitive interface. First, however, we will address a few digital topics before jumping into using Painter.

SYSTEM REQUIREMENTS

Painter runs on all Macintosh II, Performa, Centris, Quadra, and Power Macintosh series computers. While this is true, performance on 68020- and some 68030-based computers (most Macintosh II and Performa models) may be slower than you desire. The speed of any Macintosh will benefit from the installation of an accelerator board.

System Software

Painter needs 32-bit QuickDraw to operate, so you'll need Apple System 6.0.5 or later, and Painter supports System 7.0 or later.

Memory

Painter will run with 5 MB of application RAM, although not terribly efficiently. Fractal Design Corporation recommends 6 MB for 680x0 machines and 8 MB for Power Macs. We recommend 12 to 16 MB—or more if you'll be working with more than one file at a time or if you plan to run other programs (such as Photoshop) at the same time you are running Painter. For a couple of special effects, you'll need a floating-point unit (FPU).

The Painter application takes up only about 4.6 MB on your hard drive, and brushes, textures, and other related files can add another 10 MB or so.

Your art files can get *very* large—some of the art files used in this book are well over 10 MB *each*. It may sound a bit flippant, but use the same rule of thumb for hard disk space as for RAM: as much as you can afford.

If you plan on sending large graphics files to a service bureau or printer for output, you may want to investigate the necessity of a high-volume transportable system, such as a cartridge drive (44 MB or 88 MB, by SyQuest), Bernoulli drive (44 MB or 90 MB, by Iomega), floptical drive (a high-capacity floppy disk using laser technology), or an optical drive. Before purchasing a transportable media drive, please check with your service bureau to make sure it supports the system you plan to purchase.

Display

A color monitor is recommended, but Painter also works well with a gray-scale monitor. Painter is designed to run with a 24-bit color board (16 million colors), but an 8-bit board (256 colors) produces adequate results with some *dithering* (pixellation) of the image. If you are a perfectionist and want to see very accurate on-screen results, spring for the 24-bit board. Painter's screen redraw is slower on any monitor with less than a 24 bit board.

Input Devices

You can create wonderful art using your mouse or a standard tablet, but Painter supports the use of Wacom, CalComp, Summagraphics, Hitachi, or Kurta pressure-sensitive graphics tablets. If you shop around, you can find a tablet for less than $300, and we highly recommend using one. Although you can achieve most of the effects in this book using a standard tablet or a mouse, this book assumes the use of a pressure-sensitive graphics tablet.

Output Devices

There is a wide variety of output options for your Painter files, from simple black-and-white laser prints to film output for process color printing and color prints on a color laser copier or an Iris printer. Some color printers even support diverse media, so your painting can be output directly onto water color paper or canvas. Some of these output options are addressed in Chapter 11.

INSTALLING PAINTER

Installing Painter is as easy as it gets. In fact, this type of installation is sometimes referred to as a "forehead" installation: You simply bang your forehead on the keyboard a couple of times, and you're up and running.

To install Painter, create a folder labeled "Painter 3.0." Do not install Painter 3.0 in a folder containing older versions of Painter. Restart your Mac while holding down the **Shift** key to shut off any extensions you may have.

Insert the floppy disk labeled **Installer—Disk 1** into your floppy disk drive. Double-click on the Painter **Installer** icon, then select the **Painter 3.0** folder as the installation location. Click **Install into "Painter 3.0"**. Follow the prompts to insert the other floppy disks, and you're done!

LAUNCHING PAINTER

To launch Painter, simply double-click on the Painter application icon. You see the screen displayed in Figure 1.1.

LAUNCHING FOR THE FIRST TIME

If this is the first time you are launching Painter, you will be asked to personalize your software, as shown in Figure 1.2. Enter your name and the serial number (found on the back of Installer—Disk 1 or on the READ ME FIRST card), and click **OK**. If you are updating from an earlier version, you must use the *new* serial number found in your upgrade package. Painter 3.0 rejects any Painter 2.0 serial numbers.

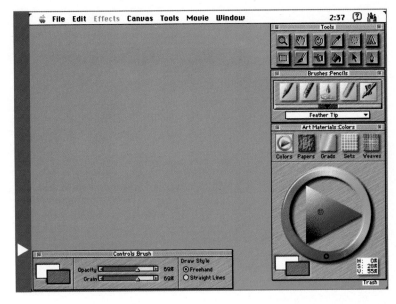

FIGURE 1.1

The Painter screen.

5

The dialog box shown in Figure 1.3 is displayed for selection of third-party, Photoshop-compatible, plug-in modules. For Painter to utilize plug-ins they must all be in in one folder. Plug-ins provide special effects and additional file formats. If you want to use any plug-ins with Painter, use this dialog box to locate them on your hard drive, and click **Open**. If you do not want to select any plug-ins right now, click **Cancel**.

To add plug-ins at a later date, select **Plug-Ins** from the fly-out **Preferences** option on the Edit menu.

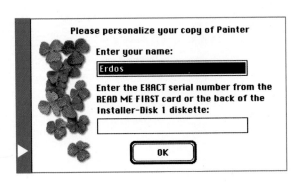

FIGURE 1.2

Personalizing your software.

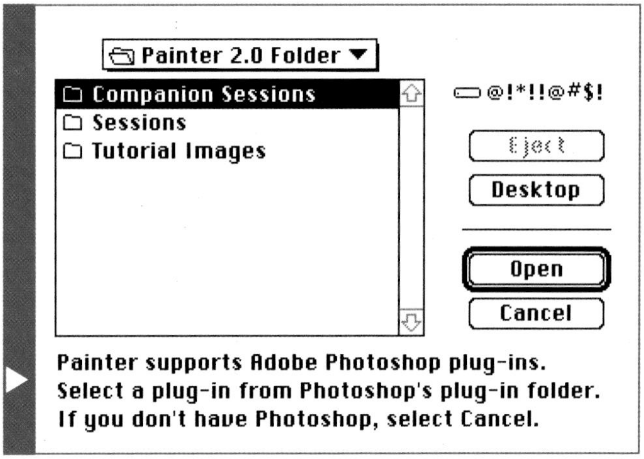

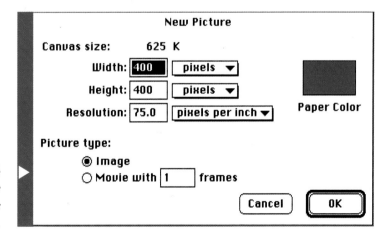

FIGURE 1.3

Selecting Photoshop-compatible plug-in modules.

TECHNICAL SUPPORT

Some older versions of INIT and DEV files can conflict with Painter. If you are experiencing trouble installing or launching Painter, call Painter's support line at (408) 688-8800 between 8 am and 5 pm Pacific time, Monday through Friday. You may also reach tech support via CompuServe (Go **FRACTAL**) or America Online (Keyword: **FRACTAL**).

Fractal Design Corp. is one of the few remaining software companies that offer free unlimited tech support, and their support staff is knowledgeable and, well, very supportive. We encourage you to take advantage of this.

FIGURE 1.4

The New Picture Size dialog box.

STARTING A WORK SESSION

Once Painter is launched, you can create a new file or work from an existing one. Painter uses many standard menu and dialog box options for opening and saving files.

To start a new file, select **New** from the File menu. The New Picture dialog box, shown in Figure 1.4, is displayed.

Enter the width and height for your image in the **Width** and **Height** fields and select the units of measurement from the pop-up menus. The default settings are for a standard 13-inch monitor.

Press **Tab** to move from one field to another. Click and hold on the pop-up menus to display your measurement choices, then drag to make a selection.

The resolution setting in this dialog box specifies pixels per inch displayed on your monitor, as well as the dots per inch (dpi) rendered by your printer. Many artists work using 75 or 150 pixels per inch, then increase the resolution for output. This saves disk space and time while working—smaller files use less RAM and process faster.

The figure next to **Canvas Size**: lets you know how much memory your file is using. Reducing the width, height, or resolution results in a smaller image size: increasing them results in a larger image size.

Click on the square above **Paper Color** to select the paper background color for your image. The standard Apple color selector, shown in Figure 1.5, is displayed.

7

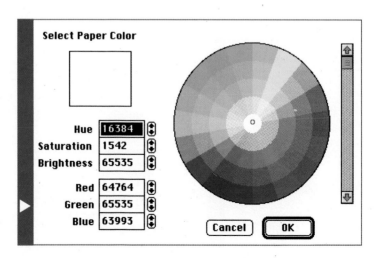

FIGURE 1.5

The standard Apple color selector.

Select your background color by entering values or clicking on the color wheel. Click **OK**. The background color is now displayed in the Paper Color window. If you are creating a still image, click on the **Image** radio button. If you are creating a movie or animation, select the **Movie with ____ frames** radio button and enter the number of frames in the corresponding field. (Please see Chapter 10 for more information on movies and animation.)

Click **OK** and a new window is opened. Your canvas is ready, and you're all set to paint.

SAVING A WORK SESSION

To save your work, select **Save** from the File menu. The Save dialog box, shown in Figure 1.6, is displayed.

Select the location for your art files and enter a file name in the **Save Image As** field.

This dialog box also gives you several file format options:

▼ **RIFF** (raster image file format). This is the *default* option. Select the RIFF format to toggle the **Uncompressed** option. To save file space, always leave the **Uncompressed** option unchecked.

▼ **TIFF** (tagged image file format). A versatile graphics format that stores a map specifying the location and color associated with each pixel. You can now choose to save an alpha channel with a TIFF using the **"Save Mask Layer"** check box. TIFF is supported by IBM-compatible and NeXT systems.

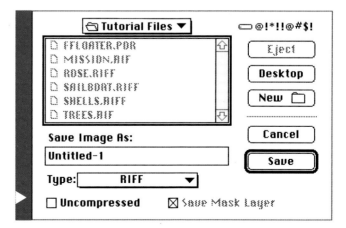

FIGURE 1.6

The Save dialog box.

8

▼ **PICT** Collections of QuickDraw routines needed to create an image. It is the main format used by the Macintosh clipboard.

▼ **Photoshop** The native file format for Adobe Photoshop files. Photoshop files are always saved in 24-bit color.

▼ **BMP** Bitmap files are the main format used by the Microsoft Windows (IBM-compatible computers) clipboard.

▼ **PCX** (picture exchange). A PC format used by many scanners and paint-style programs.

▼ **Targa** A file format used by high-end, PC-based paint programs. Targa files can have 8, 16, or 32 bits per pixel.

▼ **EPS** (Encapsulated PostScript). Painter's EPS files conform to the EPS-DCS 5 file format, used for desktop color separation. Please note that files saved in this format *cannot be reopened* by Painter. If you want to reopen a file saved in this format, save it in another format first (with another name) *before* saving it as an EPS file.

Selecting **EPS** opens the EPS Save As Options dialog box, shown in Figure 1.7.

▲ Hex (ASCII) *picture data*. Select this option for programs, such as PageMaker, that require it.

9

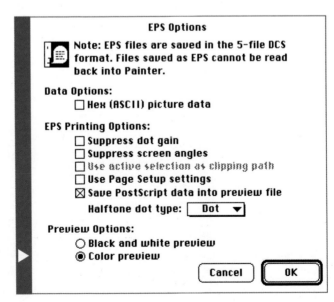

FIGURE 1.7

The EPS Save As Options dialog box.

▲ *Suppress dot gain.* This option disables Painter's dot gain adjustment.

▲ *Suppress screen angles.* This option disables Painter's screen angle adjustment.

▲ *Use active selection as clipping path.* Select this option to save only the portion of an image inside a selection. A selection must be active for this option to be enabled. Currently this feature is disabled.

▲ *Use Page Setup settings.* This option disables Painter's default printer settings: 133 lpi, standard screen angles, and 16 percent dot gain.

▲ *Save PostScript data into preview file.* This option saves a printable preview of your EPS document. This is necessary if you plan to view a composite proof before outputting to film. When this option is selected, the radio buttons for color or black-and-white previews are enabled.

▲ *Halftone dot type.* Select a dot, line, ellipse, or custom shape for your halftone screen grid. The **Custom** option lets you create your own shape using a PostScript command. You must know the PostScript programming language to do this.

After mulling over this list and selecting your file format, click **OK** to save your work. If this file format list confuses you, don't worry; you can always select **Save As** to change your file type.

OPENING AN EXISTING WORK SESSION

You may open files saved in any of the formats listed previously (except EPS), which makes it easy to work

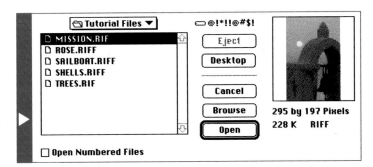

FIGURE 1.8
The File Open dialog box.

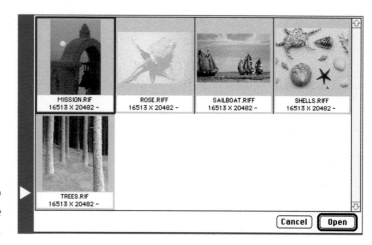

FIGURE 1.9

Browsing the contents of a folder.

with files that have been modified in other programs (such as Photoshop, ColorStudio, or Sketcher). Please note, however, that files must be saved in RGB color format to be opened in Painter.

To open an existing file, select **Open** from the File menu. The dialog box shown in Figure 1.8 is displayed. Locate the file you want to open. If the file was saved using Painter, Sketcher, or Dabbler, you'll see a thumbnail preview in the right side of this dialog box.

Below the preview window, you'll see file information for every document (even those not created in Painter): file dimension in pixels, how much memory it takes up, and its file type.

Click on **Browse** to display thumbnails of all Painter and Sketcher files in the folder you currently have selected, as shown in Figure 1.9.

The **Open Numbered Files** option automatically creates a Painter Frame Stack from sequentially numbered files to generate a Painter movie. Please see Chapter 10 for more information on this feature.

To open a file from the main File Open dialog box or from the Browse dialog box, select the file and click **Open** or double-click on your selection.

You're now ready to pick up your tools and start painting!

The Tools
Palette

CHAPTER 2

Painter is very simple and straightforward to use, yet it also has many complex and sophisticated features. Part of its ease of use lies in the simplicity of the Tools palette.

INTRODUCTION TO THE TOOLS PALETTE

Painter's Tools palette should be displayed in the upper right of your screen when you launch the program. If it's not, select **Tools** from the Windows menu.

THE CONTROLS PALETTE

To select any tool on the Tools palette, simply click on it once. The Controls palette works hand-in-hand with the Tools palette. Each time you select a tool, the Controls palette changes to reflect the currently selected tool. Sometimes the Controls palette offers information (such as the RGB values for a selected color); other times it also

offers pop-up menus, sliders, or radio buttons for fine-tuning a tool. You'll get a better feel for this as we go through each tool on the Tools palette.

Let's look at these palettes, shown in Figure 2.1.

MAGNIFIER TOOL

 The **Magnifier** tool lets you zoom in on the tiniest detail of your painting, and with a few clicks of the mouse, you can zoom out to view your composition as if you were standing across the room—all while you're parked in your chair!

Click on the **Magnifier** tool to select it. Place your cursor over the area you want to zoom in on. Notice your cursor changes to a magnifying glass with a plus sign (**+**) in the middle when you move it over your active window. Click once, and Painter magnifies the area. The magnification factors

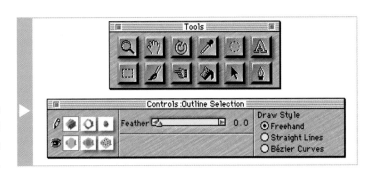

FIGURE 2.1

The Tools palette (top) and the Controls palette (bottom).

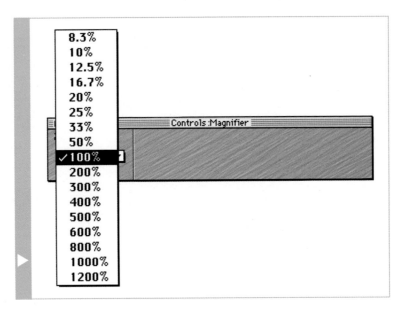

8.3%
10%
12.5%
16.7%
20%
25%
33%
50%
✓100%
200%
300%
400%
500%
600%
800%
1000%
1200%

Controls :Magnifier

FIGURE 2.2

Painter's zoom factors.

15

progress in the same increments as under the **Zoom Level** option on the Controls palette (from 8.3 percent to 1,200 percent), as shown in Figure 2.2.

The magnification factor is indicated in the title bar of your window; for example, it may say **Untitled @ 200%**.

To zoom out, place your cursor in the active window, and hold down the **Option** key. Notice the plus sign in the magnifying glass cursor changes to a minus sign (–). Click in the area you want to reduce. Your image zooms out in the same increments that it zoomed in. You can also click and drag with the **Magnifier** tool to zoom into a particular area.

GRABBER TOOL

 The **Grabber** tool is used to move your image around in a window—just grab it and move.

To use the **Grabber** tool, select it, then click and drag the cursor in your window. Release the mouse or stylus.

ROTATE PAGE TOOL

 The **Rotate Page** tool was developed to accommodate artists who are used to turning a page as they work. With this tool selected, click on the page you want to rotate. You'll see a large box with an arrow in it.

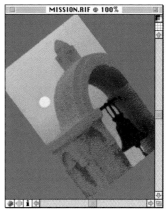

FIGURE 2.3

Using the Rotate Page tool.

Drag your cursor to rotate the arrow in the direction you want your page to turn, then release the cursor button. To return to your regular upright view, simply click once on the image while the **Rotate Page** tool is selected. Figure 2.3 shows the **Rotate Page** tool in action.

(Clicking on the **Colors** icon toggles the extended palette on and off.) There are two rectangles on the lower left of the palette—make sure the front one is selected, as in Figure 2.4.

Move your cursor, now shaped like a dropper, over the source area for your

DROPPER TOOL

The **Dropper** tool lets you select a color from a painted area to use on another area. You can even use it to get a color from another open file.

When you use the **Dropper** tool, make sure the Foreground indicator for the Colors option is selected on the Art Materials palette.

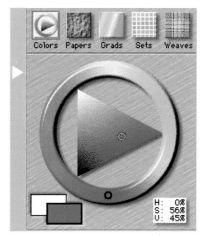

FIGURE 2.4

Activating the foreground color on the Art Materials palette. The overlapping rectangles are also visible on the Controls palette.

color, and click once. Your color is now shown in the foreground rectangle on your Color palette. Now you can select a brush and paint with the selected color.

TEXT SELECTION TOOL

 The **Text Selection** tool adds text to your images, as in Figure 2.5. You may work with text selections as you would with other selections. Chapter 7 covers text selection in greater detail.

SELECTION TOOLS

 You guessed it—the **Rectangular Selection** and **Oval Selection** tools let you select areas of your painting.

Double-clicking on the **Rectangular Selection** tool selects all of the image. Or choose **Select All** (**Command+A**) from the Edit menu to select the entire image.

Click and drag over the area you wish to select. To deselect an area, choose **Deselect** from the Edit menu, or press **Command+D**. Double-clicking on the **Selection** tool also deselects any area.

To adjust the boundaries of a selected area, hold down the **Shift** key and click and drag on the selection marquee, as shown in Figure 2.6.

The Rectangular Selection tool does not create paths that appear in the P.List but the Oval Selection tool does. Chapter 7 covers many of the options you can use on a selected area.

BRUSHES TOOL

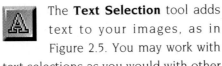 Here's where the action is. Select the **Brushes** tool to access your painting and drawing tools. Please note that unlike most paint programs, this simply places you in painting mode; specific

17

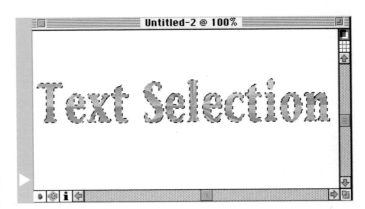

FIGURE 2.5

Adding a text selection.

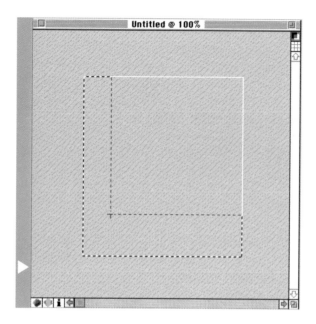

FIGURE 2.6

*Adjusting the boundaries
of a selected area.*

painting and drawing tools are selected from the Brushes palette (coming
up soon), not from the Tools palette.

FLOATING SELECTION TOOL

 Floating selections are selections
that are turned into objects you
can move, manipulate, and save
for later use. Chapter 7 covers floating
selections in greater detail.

FILL TOOL

The **Fill** tool, often referred to as
the **Bucket** tool, lets you apply
color to a selected area. This

tool is covered in detail in Chapter 5,
"Using Color."

THE OUTLINE SELECTION AND
PATH ADJUSTER TOOLS

The **Outline Selection** tool
draws freehand and Beziér
paths, either freehand or restricted to
straight lines. The **Path Adjuster** tool
lets you activate and edit any paths you
many have added to your image. Paths
in Painter work in a similar fashion to
paths in popular drawing programs,
such as Illustrator or Freehand, with the
added advantage of being attached to
the rest of Painter's features. Paths are
covered in detail in Chapter 7.

Brushes and Paint

CHAPTER 3

This chapter covers the fundamentals of Painter's Brushes and Art Materials palettes—the backbone of the program—and lets you get right into painting. After reading this chapter, you should be able to select colors, paint, and draw with any paintbrush or drawing tool.

THE BRUSHES PALETTE

This is the part you've been waiting for! Get out an old art supplies catalogue, and look at all of the tools you can't afford to buy. Now sit down at your computer and blink your eyes like Barbara Eden in I *Dream of Jeannie*—they're all here …and then some.

To get started, make sure your Brushes palette is displayed. If it's not, select **Brushes** from the Windows menu, or press **Command+2**. Select your **Brush** tool from the Tools palette, choose a brush from the Brushes palette, shown in Figure 3.1, and you're ready to go.

The Brushes palette displays five choices, but you actually have many more to choose from than that. To see the full palette, click on the drawer arrow (directly beneath the middle brush). To close the drawer, click on the arrow a second time. The Brushes palette is shown in Figure 3.2 with its drawer in the open position.

Each major tool group (chalk, water colors, oil paints, pens, etc.), represented on the Brushes palette by colorful icons, has choices of variants, such as brush sizes and types, available on the pop-up menu on the very bottom of the palette. This section describes the major tool groups and their variants. You also have an enormous array of customization choices to apply to these tools. Since that's a more complex and advanced subject, we'll cover it in Chapter 4, "Customizing Your Brushes."

To select a tool group, click on it once or select it from the pop-up menu in the drawer (it's the second from the bottom, next to the **Library** button). To select a variant, click on the variant pop-up menu, and drag to the selection you want, as shown in Figure 3.3. Release the mouse or stylus to

FIGURE 3.1

The Brushes palette with its drawer closed.

FIGURE 3.2

The Brushes palette with its drawer open.

choose your variant. Slower computers may exhibit lag time for some tools.

The currently selected brush is shown on the top row with a red border around it. To replace a specific brush on the top row with a brush from the drawer, click on the brush in the drawer, hold down your cursor button, drag it over the brush you want to replace, and release the cursor button.

USING THE CONTROLS PALETTE WITH BRUSHES

You can adjust the amount of intensity a brush has (**Opacity**), as well as how it interacts with paper grain (**Grain**) by adjusting the respective sliders on the Controls palette.

▼ **Opacity** works in two ways:

▲ *Buildup method brushes.* Move this slider left to keep your colors truer to the color on

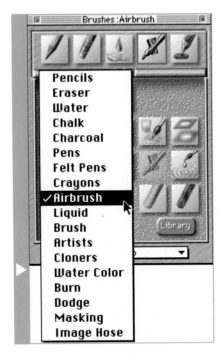

FIGURE 3.3

Selecting a variant on the Brushes palette.

21

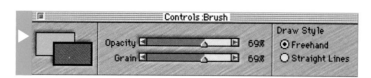

FIGURE 3.4

The Controls palette for Brushes.

your palette, or right to let them muddy up quicker.

▲ *Cover brushes.* Move this slider left for more transparent coverage, or right for more opaque coverage.

▼ **Grain** controls the amount of color that penetrates the paper when you use grainy method brushes. Move the slider left (less paper grain shows) or right (more paper grain shows) to adjust this setting.

In version 2.0, **Opacity** was known as **Concentration**, and **Grain** was known as **Penetration**. Figure 3.4 shows the Controls palette for Brushes.

THE EXPANDED BRUSHES PALETTE

The Brushes palette is also expandable. Click on the zoom box in the upper-right corner, and

more (can you believe it!) options become available: Method Category, Method Subcategory, and Library. Figure 3.5 shows an expanded Brushes palette.

▼ **Method Category and Subcategory.** This decides the nature of the brush stroke and is probably the most important part of customizing your tools. If you click on the pop-

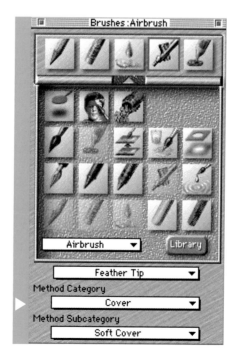

FIGURE 3.5

An expanded Brushes palette.

up menus, it seems pretty intimidating, but it is really organized quite well, and is actually easy and fun to use. It is covered in detail in Chapter 4, "Customizing Brushes."

▼ **Library.** When you create custom variants—also covered in Chapter 4—you'll definitely want to save them (well, most of them). This feature lets you access saved custom brush libraries.

Remember, like their traditional counterparts, these digital tools react to the surface to which you apply them. Chapter 6, "Scratching the Surface," dips further into this subject.

Unlike their traditional counterparts, you can combine media you never dreamed of, such as placing chalk over a layer of oil paints, erasing felt pens, or using masks and selections with any medium. Take your rule book, throw it out, and write your own.

Pencils

 Pencils react very well to canvas or paper surfaces, as well as to stylus pressure. If you are using a mouse or standard stylus, you can adjust pencil pressure by moving the **Grain** slider left (lighter) or right (darker) before stroking.

 2B Pencil. A thin, soft-lead pencil.

 500 lb. Pencil. This quarter-ton monster generates (boy, does it generate) fat lines. *Very* fat.

 Colored Pencils. This produces the same effect as traditional colored pencils.

 Sharp Pencil. A thin, hard-lead pencil.

 Single Pixel Scribbler. The antithesis of the **500 lb. Pencil**, this produces one-pixel lines—as thin as they get.

Thick & Thin Pencils. This has the same effect as drawing with both the sharpened tip and the flat edge of pencil lead. It creates lines that vary from thick to thin, depending on the direction in which you are drawing.

Eraser

Oh %#@!!*&$!!! You just made a mistake. Not a big deal—just erase it. Painter offers three kinds of erasers, all pressure-sensitive:

Eraser Variants. These erase right down to the paper color chosen when the document was created. Eraser variants come in five flavors: **Flat Eraser**, **Fat Eraser**, **Medium Eraser**, **Small Eraser**, and **Ultrafine Eraser**.

 Bleach Erasers. Just like Clorox, these variants erase to white, regardless of the paper color. They are available in **Fat Bleach**, **Medium Bleach**, **Small Bleach**, **Ultrafine Bleach**, and **Single Pixel Bleach**.

24

 Eraser Darkeners. There was a little bit of liberty taken when they named these variants erasers: **Darkeners** actually *increase* the density of the image. Choose from **Fat Darkener**, **Medium Darkener**, **Small Darkener**, and **Ultrafine Darkener**.

Water

 Use the **Water** tools to smudge areas created by other tools or to dilute strokes made by any other tool.

 Big Frosty Water. Works like **Frosty Water**, at about two or three times the width.

 Frosty Water. Smears with a harder edge than **Just Add Water** while retaining some texture.

 Grainy Water. Use this when you want to retain and work with paper texture. It is also useful for adding texture to smooth areas.

 Just Add Water. This variant smudges with smooth, clean strokes. Be careful, though, because it removes paper grain while it smudges.

 Single Pixel Water. An itsy-bitsy smear of water, this is like dragging a wet thread through your image.

 Tiny Frosty Water. Works like **Frosty Water,** at about half the width.

 Water Rake. Produces the effect of dragging a wet, hard-bristled brush through your image.

Water Spray. Sprays water onto your image, as if you were using an aspirator.

Chalk

 More like traditional pastels than chalk, these tools are the favorite choice of many artists. You can get some amazing effects when you use the **Chalk** tools with paper textures and the **Water** tools.

 Artist Pastel Chalk. This variant creates an opaque chalk stroke.

 Large Chalk. Works like **Artist Pastel Chalk** at about twice the width.

 Oil Pastel Chalk. This variant slightly smears the stroke beneath it.

 Sharp Chalk. Works like **Artist Pastel Chalk**, at about half the width.

 Square Chalk. Works like **Artist Pastel Chalk**, with a sharp, straight edge.

Charcoal

 Like traditional charcoal, this tool is great for sketching out your composition, but here you get 16 million colors and no dust. Charcoal produces a more opaque stroke than chalk.

 Default. A more textured variant of this tool.

 Gritty Charcoal. Produces a rich stroke that varies in width according to the direction of the stroke, as if you were alternating between the flat edge and the point of the charcoal.

 Soft Charcoal. A textured variant of this tool, using very soft strokes.

Pens

 An incredible assortment of pens with no clogging, no ink jars, and no splattering (unless, of course, you *want* splattering).

 Calligraphy. Fine hand lettering is now a breeze! Select this option for incredible calligraphic strokes.

Fine Point. This tool works just like a ball point pen.

 Flat Color. A cousin to the **500 lb. Pencil**, this lays down an oversized, opaque stroke.

 Leaky Pen. The longer you drag, the bigger the leak. Careful, you don't want to get this all over your shirt.

 Pen and Ink. A very opaque, smooth stroke.

 Pixel Dust. Not exactly like any pen we've ever used, this tool sprays fairy dust all over your image.

 Scratchboard Rake. We call this one sgraffito with a cat's claw.

 Scratchboard Tool. Scraffito made fast and easy. For loads of fun, set your paper color to black, and scratch away.

Single Pixel. A single-pixel pen, unaffected by stylus pressure.

 Smooth Ink Pen. This variant works like a fountain pen, with greater pressure creating a thicker stroke, and less pressure creating a thinner stroke.

Felt Pens

 No, these pressure-sensitive pens won't dry out if you leave the caps off. And they're great for comps, cartoons, and caricatures.

 Dirty Marker. A much darker and muddier version of the **Felt Marker**. The nib of this pen is wider for horizontal strokes than for vertical strokes.

 Felt Marker. A much softer and transparent version of the **Felt Tip** variants. The nib of this pen is wider for horizontal strokes than for vertical strokes.

 Fine Tip Felt Pens. Press as hard as you want, this narrow pen won't tear your paper.

 Medium Tip Felt Pens. About twice the width of the **Fine Tip** pen, and very opaque.

26

Single Pixel Marker. Finer than any pen we've ever used, this marker produces a *very* thin stroke.

Crayons

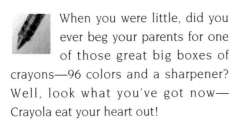 When you were little, did you ever beg your parents for one of those great big boxes of crayons—96 colors and a sharpener? Well, look what you've got now—Crayola eat your heart out!

Like their traditional counterparts, these strokes get darker as you layer them; in fact, they can get downright muddy. Press as hard as you want—they won't break.

 Default. Plain and simple, this is a crayon.

 Waxy Crayons. Did you ever put your crayons on the radiator, then try to draw with them? Well, now you can do it but without getting grounded for a week. Melt away.

Airbrush

 This tool lays down gradual tones of color, with a very soft edge to your strokes, as if you were using a traditional airbrush or spray can, with none of those CFCs or fumes. As with most other tools, increasing stylus pressure or **Opacity** increases the opacity of your coverage.

 Fat Stroke. A thick, soft, semi-transparent stroke, good for covering large areas.

 Feather Tip. Lays down soft, thin lines with greater opacity than the **Fat Stroke** or **Thin Stroke** variants.

 Single Pixel Air. A very fine **Airbrush** variant.

 Spatter Airbrush. A very textured, transparent, and thick-stroked variant that reacts well to paper texture.

 Thin Stroke. Produces the same coverage as the **Fat Stroke**, at about one-quarter of the stroke width.

Liquid

 Most **Liquid** variants smear more than they paint. You can get effects that range from using oil paints with a palette knife to dragging a wet brush through your image to good old-fashioned finger painting. Use these variants for both

27

applying new paint and adding effects to existing images. To move or smear paint without adding color, reduce your **Opacity** slider to **0 percent**.

 Coarse Distorto. A more textured, less smooth version of the **Distorto** variant.

 Coarse Smeary Bristles. Like **Smeary Bristles**, but with a larger stroke and more texture.

 Coarse Smeary Mover. Moves existing paint around with a coarser texture than the **Smeary Mover**.

 Distorto. A very wet, smooth tool that moves, more than smears, existing paint. Very cool.

 Smeary Bristles. A very texture-sensitive and pressure-sensitive tool that smears color from your color palette onto your image.

 Smeary Mover. Basically the same tool as the **Smeary Bristles**, but with **Opacity** set to **0 percent** so that it moves existing paint around, rather than adding new paint.

 Thick Oil. A very thick, very opaque wet brush loaded with oily paint.

 Tiny Smudge. A small, textured smudging tool. The default setting has the **Opacity** set at **0 percent** so that no color is applied from the Color palette. To add color to this tool, move the **Opacity** slider to the right.

 Total Oil Brush. Creates a thinner stroke than the **Smeary Bristles**.

Brush

 Although all of the tools on the Brushes palette are called "brushes," this is where the more traditional brushes—oil and acrylic brushes—reside.

Please note that these brushes always cover the paint they overlay, even if your **Opacity** is set to a lower percentage. Setting the **Opacity** of these brushes to **0 percent** doesn't make the paint more translucent—it simply doesn't apply paint.

 Big Loaded Oils is a broader version of the **Loaded Oils** brush.

Big Rough Out. A larger, more textured version of the **Rough Out** variant.

 Big Wet Oils is a broad-stroked brush that mixes its color with the color of the paint beneath it.

 Brushy is a multibristled brush that mixes with the colors it is dragged through and runs out of paint at the end of a stroke.

 Camel Hair Brush. A softer oil brush than the **Oil Paint** variant. Slower strokes give the effect of having your bristles closer together, faster strokes spread the bristles. The width of your stroke is reduced with less stylus pressure and increased with greater stylus pressure.

 Coarse Hairs is a multi-bristled, coarse-bristled brush.

 Cover Brush. A soft, very slightly textured brush. Increased stylus pressure increases stroke width and opacity.

 Digital Sumi. A multiple-bristled sumi brush, with a rake-like effect. Increased stylus pressure increases stroke width.

 Fine Brush is a multibristled, fine-bristled brush.

 Graduated Brush. A thinner oil-type brush that uses two colors, depending on the amount of pressure on your stylus. The colors are taken from the two rectangles on your Color palette: the primary color is selected in the front rectangle, the secondary color is selected in the back rectangle. Greater pressure adds more of your primary color, while less pressure increases your secondary color.

 Hairy Brush. Your regular bristle brush. The stroke width and grain of this oil-like variant is determined by the amount of pressure placed on your stylus—less pressure creates thinner strokes with less penetration, more pressure creates thicker strokes with greater penetration. Wait until each stroke is rendered by your computer, or else you'll end up with dots rather than strokes.

 Huge Rough Out. A larger, more textured version of the **Big Rough Out** variant.

 Loaded Oils is a multicolored oil brush.

 Oil Paint. Produces an oil-paint effect using a hard-bristled brush. This variant has very hard edges, and the width of your stroke is reduced with less stylus pressure and increased with greater stylus pressure. **Grain** and **Opacity** are increased with greater stylus pressure.

 Penetration Brush. This variant works like acrylics and reacts well to surface texture. Slower strokes give the effect of having your bristles closer together, faster strokes spread the bristles.

 Rough Out. Named because it is a good brush to use to cre-

ate rough, textured images; slower strokes with this dry brush variant increase the width of your stroke, while faster strokes decrease the width.

 Sable Chisel Tip Water is a fine-bristled brush that simulates the smearing effect of painting water onto an image.

 Small Loaded Oils is a thinner version of the **Loaded Oils** brush.

 Smaller Water Brush is a thin, fine-bristled brush that smears the selected color into the existing paint layer.

 Ultrafine Water Brush works just like the Smaller Water Brush, but with a larger number of smaller bristles.

Artists

 These variants give you the ability to paint using the brush types of the old masters. Increased stylus pressure increases opacity, and faster strokes produce thinner widths.

Auto Van Gogh. This is another way to get Impressionistic results. The **Auto Van Gogh** variant works using a clone, and is explained in Chapter 8, "Cloning and Scanned Images."

 Flemish Rub. Another take on the **Impressionist** variant, **Flemish Rub** smears existing paint to produce an Impressionistic effect on an existing image.

 Impressionist. It's easy to emulate the French Impressionists with this tool. Increased opacity adds more color, reduced opacity spreads existing paint.

 Piano Keys. This brush variant generates a multicolored stroke that looks like a ribbon of piano keys.

 Seurat. This variant gives you the pointillist (dabs of pure color to produce intense color effects) technique developed by Georges Seurat.

 Van Gogh. If you use the Impressionist color palette, strokes from this brush give you the multicolored effect used by Vincent Van Gogh. The **Van Gogh** tool hides underlying strokes, regardless of the **Opacity** setting. Short strokes work best with this variant. For each stroke, a dotted line is displayed while the image is being rendered. Wait for your computer to completely render the stroke before beginning your next stroke, or you'll end up with dots rather than lines.

Cloners

 Cloner brushes let you take an existing image (usually a scanned photograph) and apply different types of media to them. You select a default clone setting, and Painter provides color information while you control how the brush strokes are applied. Cloners are covered in detail in Chapter 8, "Cloning and Scanned Images," but we'll give you a brief overview of the variants here.

▼ **Chalk Cloner.** Creates the effect of the **Artist Pastel Chalk** variant.

▼ **Driving Rain Cloner.** Creates an image that looks like it is being seen through a window in the rain.

▼ **Felt Pen Cloner.** Adds strokes from a felt tip pen. The darkness (or "dirtiness") of the strokes increases as you lay more down.

▼ **Hairy Cloner.** Produces strokes that emulate the **Hairy Brush** variant of the brush.

▼ **Hard Oil Cloner.** Lays down hard-edged oil-paint strokes that cover underlying paint.

▼ **Impressionist Cloner.** Paints with the short, multicolored strokes found in the **Impressionist** variant of the Artist brush.

▼ **Melt Cloner.** "Melts" an image by painting with strokes similar to the **Distorto** variant of the Liquid brush.

▼ **Oil Brush Cloner.** Paints with oil-paint strokes that cover underlying paint.

▼ **Pencil Sketch Cloner.** Lays down pencil strokes.

▼ **Soft Cloner.** Creates an image in which the edges of the stokes are softer than in the original.

▼ **Straight Cloner.** Re-creates the original image.

▼ **Van Gogh Cloner.** Produces strokes that emulate the **Van Gogh** variant of the Artist brush.

Water Color

 The **Water Color** variants produce beautiful, soft, translucent images. You'll get great results if you use the pastel color set on the Art Materials: Color Sets palette. All of the **Water Color** variants react well to surface textures, except for the **Wet Eraser**.

You must select **Wet Paint** from the Canvas menu to use any of the **Water Color** tools. When you do this, you are painting on a layer that "floats" above any existing image you may have on your canvas. When you are done using your water colors, select **Dry** from the Canvas menu. This "dries" your water color layer and sends it to the underlying image layer.

The selection and mask tools do not work on a wet water color layer. To clear a wet layer, select **Dry** from the Canvas menu, then select **Undo** from the Edit menu. When you are all through using your **Water Color** variants, toggle off the **Wet Paint** selection on the Canvas menu.

Broad Water Brush. Paints with a very wide, translucent stroke that shows some bristle marks.

 Diffuse Water. Lays down a concentrated layer of paint with diffused edges. The edges diffuse after the color is laid down, as if it were being absorbed by the paper. Increased stylus pressure increases stroke width and opacity.

 Large Simple Water. A larger version of the **Simple Water** variant.

 Large Water. Lays down a very wide, lightly colored, translucent layer of paint.

 Pure Water Brush. This brush adds water (with no color added) to your image.

 Simple Water. Your basic water color stroke, without bristles. Adding layers of colors using this variant produces a smooth, blended effect.

Spatter Water. This variant splatters colored drops of water onto your image, as if you were flicking your brush.

 Water Brush Stroke. Your basic water color stroke, showing bristle marks. Increased stylus pressure increases stroke width. Wait until each stroke is rendered before beginning another stroke.

 Wet Eraser. Use this variant to erase water color strokes on the "floating" layer of wet paint.

Burn

 Burn increases the saturation of color of the image to which you apply it. This tool increases the color of the image without being affected by the color selected on your color palette.

Dodge

 The opposite of **Burn**, this variant fades the color from an image. The color selected on your color palette does not affect the way **Dodge** fades an image.

MASKING

 Masking brushes allow you to paint in or paint away the mask on a floater or image using brush strokes. Masking is covered in detail in Chapter 7, but for now, we'll give you a brief overview of the variants:

▼ **Big Masking Pen** masks with wide, smooth lines that do not react to the paper texture.

▼ **Grainizer** masks with very grainy strokes, based on the currently selected paper texture.

▼ **Masking Airbrush** masks with a soft, sprayed effect as you would expect from an airbrush.

▼ **Masking Chalk** masks with grainy lines that react to the selected paper grain.

▼ **Masking Pen** masks with smooth lines that do not react to the paper texture.

▼ **Single Pixel Masking Pen** masks with smooth, single-pixel lines.

IMAGE HOSE

 The Image Hose paints with complete images, not just pigments, spraying the images across your canvas. The Image Hose variants control the way your images—known as *Nozzles*—flow from the brush. They are grouped according to feature:

▼ **Directional** variants work similar to linear variants, placing images on your canvas in single-file.

▼ **Linear** places images on your canvas in a single line that follows the placement of your cursor.

▼ **Random** places multiple images on your canvas in a random fashion.

▼ **Sequential** places multiple elements on your canvas in a sequential fashion.

▼ **Size** refers to the spacing between elements: **Small**, **Medium**, and **Large**.

▼ **Spray** randomly places images on your canvas as if they had been sprayed on.

This very neat feature is covered in detail in Chapter 9.

Once you select the tool group and variant you want to paint with, paint. Really. That's it.

THE COLOR PALETTE

Sixteen million colors. We'll say it again: 16 *million colors*. And you'll never run out of them.

FIGURE 3.6

*Selecting a color from the **Colors** icon on the Art Materials palette.*

the dominant hue in the triangular color picker. The triangle exhibits the saturation and value of the hue selected on the spectrum slider. Use the selection circle to select saturation and brightness by sliding it around in the triangle.

Or choose from one of the existing default color sets. To change to a new set of color squares, click on the **Set** icon on the top of the Art Materials palette, shown in Figure 3.7.

The **Colors** icon on the Art Materials palette is your main source for selecting and creating colors. Click on the icon and the zoom box in the upper right of the palette to display the extended Colors palette, shown in Figure 3.6.

This section covers the basics of selecting and using colors. Chapter 5, "Using Color," discusses additional color topics.

Click on the **Library** button and select a Color Set from the choices in the **Colors, Grads, and Weaves** folder, then click **Open**. The selected palette is displayed. Simply click on a color to use it.

SELECTING COLORS

Use a combination of the spectrum ring and the triangular color picker to create your colors. The spectrum ring selects

Saving Color Sets

The ability to create new color sets gives you the flexibility to create custom palettes for projects, clients, and more.

35

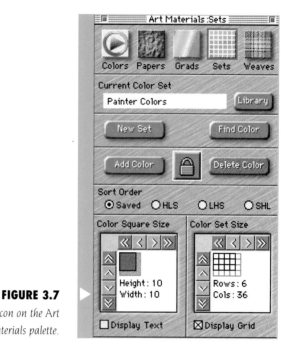

FIGURE 3.7

*Selecting a Color Set from the **Set** icon on the Art Materials palette.*

To permanently save new colors, you have to create a new set. If you want to add colors from an existing image using the **Dropper** tool, make sure the image is open before creating a new set.

Click on the **New Set** button and you'll see a single-item color set. Select a color from the **Color** icon or an existing image (using the **Dropper** tool), then click the **Add Color** button on the Sets palette.

You can use the same process to add to an existing color set. If the set is locked, click on the padlock icon to unlock it.

To name the set, click on the set's close box, and follow the file-naming prompts.

PRACTICE SESSION

1. All right. It's time to get down to work. Let's paint! Select **New** from the File menu. Select the default settings in the New Picture Size dialog box by pressing **Return**.

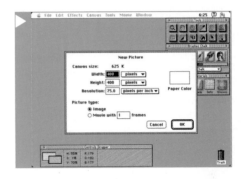

2. Select the **Sharp Pencil** variant from the Brushes palette, and **black** from the Colors palette. Now sketch the outline of a cow.

3. Select the **Artist Pastel** variant of the Chalk brush. Open the Pastels color set from the Art Materials palette, and choose a pale color for the cow's body. Start filling in your outline. Then select a darker color for shadowed areas, and apply that to the undersides of the cow.

PRACTICE SESSION CONTINUED

4. Use the **Feather Tip Airbrush** variant to add some pink to the muzzle, udder, and ears. Add some tan to the horns and the tip of the tail.

5. Airbrush some black spots on the cow, then add details to the eyes, nose, and hooves using the **Single Pixel Pen** tool.

6. Add some green grass around the cow's hooves by using the **Piano Keys** variant of the Artists brush. A bit rough, but it's a good start.

Customizing Brushes

CHAPTER 4

If after reading Chapter 3 you thought you had plenty of tools to work with, *wait* until you read this chapter. The tools we covered in Chapter 3 are simply a library of preset default brushes the folks at Fractal Design Corp. put together to make your life easier, but you can create an almost endless array of custom brushes to suit your own working style. Your choices for customization include adding variants to existing brushes or creating whole new brush categories on the Brushes palette (including their own name and icon).

CUSTOMIZING BRUSH BEHAVIOR

No, brushes can't misbehave, but their strokes can be edited and refined. Let's see how they work..

METHOD

Method determines the nature of your brush stroke. Each of the default selections in the Brushes palette already has a method assigned to it that gives it the characteristics of its traditional parallel.

A tool's method is chosen from the **Method Category** and **Method Subcategory** pop-up menus on the extended Brushes palette, shown in Figure 4.1.

Strokes are created using two sets of properties: a stroke method category plus stroke subcategories, outlined in Table 4.1.

Now you simply decide what you want in a stroke, and choose the category and subcategory that best achieve that goal. It's like ordering from a menu in a family-style restaurant: Choose one option from Column A (in this case one

FIGURE 4.1

The **Method Category** *pop-up menu (left) and the* **Method Subcategory** *pop-up menu.*

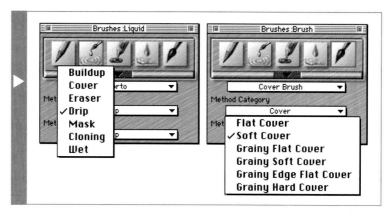

TABLE 4.1   *Stroke categories and subcategories.*

Column A
Method Categories

 Buildup methods give you brushes whose strokes "build up" on the ones under them to produce a more opaque stroke. Buildup methods tend to generate darker, muddier results. The **Felt Pens** variants use Buildup methods.

 Cover methods paint over—or cover—earlier layers of paint, instead of building on underlying layers like the Buildup methods. Rather than build up to a blacker, muddier tone, Cover methods simply become more opaque as more paint is applied.

 Eraser methods affect underlying strokes by erasing them, smearing them, or darkening them. Please note the names of these methods use terms like "Paint Thickener" and "Drip" rather than "Editing."

 Drip methods smear underlying strokes, usually resulting in a distorted effect.

 Mask methods are for painting on the mask layer for the purpose of image editing.

 Cloning methods let you clone (or copy into a new file) an existing image and regenerate it.

 Wet methods create the effects of using water color paints. Wet methods only work in the Wet Paint layer.

Column B
Method Subcategories

 Flat gives you hard-edged strokes.

 Soft produces smooth strokes.

 Grainy produces strokes that react to your paper surface.

 Hard creates rough-edged strokes.

 Edge gives you strokes with a dense edge.

 Variable creates strokes that start with more transparency.

of the method categories), and one or more from Column B (in this case the subcategories).

For example, in Figure 4.2, Grainy Hard Buildup gives you strokes that react to the paper texture (Grainy—Column B), have rough edges (Hard—Column B), that eventually build up over each other to muddier, blacker tones (Buildup—Column A). Grainy Soft Cover gives you a paper-grain sensitive (Grainy—Column B), smooth (Soft—Column B) strokes that hide underlying strokes (Cover—Column A). Getting the hang of it?

Let's try one more. Soft Grain Colorize creates paper-grain sensitive (Grainy—Column B), smooth-edged (Soft—Column B) strokes that paint with a mask. "Huh?" you may say. "Colorize isn't a category." Well, you're right.

There are a few items on the Methods pop-up menus that, due to their names, defy our little Column A/Column B system. Let's quickly mention them.

 Paper Color (Eraser method) removes paint strokes down to the original paper color.

 Paint Remover (Eraser method) removes paint and replaces it with white.

FIGURE 4.2
Examples of some methods.

Paint Thickener (Eraser method) increases the concentration of a color.

 Mask Colorize (Eraser method) paints within the mask layer from Photoshop and ColorStudio files opened in Painter.

 Wet Buildup (Wet method) produces watery strokes on the Wet Paint layer.

 Wet Abrasive (Wet method) places color over existing paint on the Wet Paint layer.

 Wet Remove Density (Wet method) is the eraser for the Wet Paint Layer.

Got it? Great! Now let's learn how to refine brush strokes even *more* using dab spacing and bristles.

BRUSH SIZE

 The width, tip, and angle of your brush strokes are controlled from the **Brush Size** icon on the Brush Controls palette. To open the palette, shown in its expanded form in Figure 4.3, select **Brush Controls (Command+4)** from the Window menu.

▼ **Stroke contour.** The six icons in the upper right of the window allow you to select the contour of a brush nib.

 Pointed. Strokes using this nib provide more color at the center than at the edges of a brush, as with the **Sharp Chalk** variant.

43

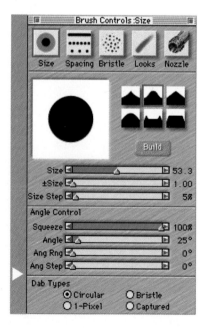

FIGURE 4.3

The Expanded Brush Controls: Size palette.

Medium. This nib produces concentrated color in the center of a stroke, as with the **Artist Chalk** variant.

 Linear. This nib gives strokes with a small area of color in the center of a stroke, as with the **Crayons**.

 Dull. This nib strokes with a moderate amount of color in the center, as with most of the **Pencil** variants.

 Watercolor. Strokes with this nib pool color at the edges, as with many of the **Watercolor** brushes.

 1-Pixel. Strokes from this nib provide flat color throughout, as with the **Calligraphy Pen** variant.

▼ **Preview window.** The preview window in the upper left of the palette displays stroke angle, width (black), and the spread of color through a stroke (gray).

▼ **Build.** Click on this button to have Painter build a brush with the options you have selected. You cannot paint with the parameters you chose without first clicking on **Build**.

▼ **Size** increases (right) or decreases (left) the width of your brush stroke.

▼ **±Size** controls the spread of color through a stroke. Move the slider left to decrease the range of a stroke width, right to increase it. When you move this slider, the black circle in the preview window shows the minimum stroke width, the gray circle shows the maximum stroke width. This feature is often used with pressure settings.

▼ **Size Step** controls the transition of a stroke from thick to thin and thin to thick. A lower percentage indicates a smoother transition, while a higher percentage provides a much more blunt transition.

▼ **Squeeze** determines the roundness of a brush. Moving this slider to the right makes a brush rounder, left makes it more elliptical.

▼ **Angle** controls the brush direction of a chosen nib. Use it with the **Thinness** option, which controls the width of the angle.

▼ **Ang Rng** selects the maximum range of angles available in a stroke. Moving this slider to 45 degrees lets a stroke range from 0 to 45 degrees.

▼ **Ang Step** controls the number of angles in a brush. A lower setting provides more brush angles, a higher setting provides fewer brush angles.

▼ **Dab Types** controls the nature of the brush dab.

DAB SPACING

Dab Spacing controls whether a brush stroke is continuous or made up of a series of dabs. This palette also controls the bristle behavior of a brush.

Open the Spacing palette, shown in Figure 4.4, by clicking the **Spacing** icon on the Brush Controls palette.

Let's take a look at these sliders.

▼ **Spacing/Size** controls the space between dabs in a brush stroke. Move the slider right to make the stroke denser and more continuous.

▼ **Min Spacing** further refines your "dab factor" by specifying the smallest number of pixels between dabs.

Real-time, multiple-bristle brushes are brushes that give you incredibly realistic oil paint and acrylic paint effects. They are most effective when used with a surface texture.

▼ **Stroke Types** determines the bristle behavior of a brush.

▲ *Single* has one path.

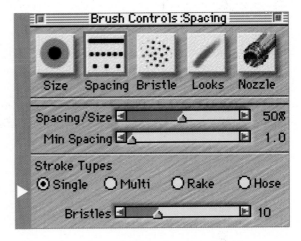

FIGURE 4.4

The expanded Brush Controls:Spacing palette.

Multi generates brushes that paint with visible bristle marks. Multiple bristles can have more than one color in a stroke.

 Rake is a fixed set of strokes that can have more than one color in a stroke.

 Hose is a single-stroke type that tells Painter to use the current Image Hose file for a stroke.

▼ **Bristles** slider works with the Stroke Types radio buttons to control the number of strokes in Multi and Rake strokes.

THE BRISTLE PALETTE

 These options, shown in Figure 4.5, let you customize existing bristle brushes or build your own. All of the default bristle brushes use the Cover method, so their strokes cover existing paint.

▼ **Thickness** controls the width of the bristle set.

▼ **Clumpiness** increases (move right) and decreases (move left) the randomness of the bristle path.

▼ **Hair Scale** determines the size of the individual bristles.

▼ **Scale/Size** increases (move right) and decreases (move left) the variability of bristle size within a stroke.

RAKE SETTINGS

The Rake palette is available from the first icon on the Advanced Controls palette, shown in Figure 4.6. These controls determine the behavior of the bristles on a Rake stroke.

▼ **Contact Angle** widens the stroke.

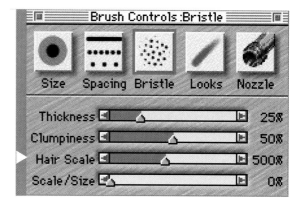

FIGURE 4.5

The Bristle palette.

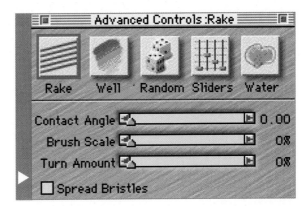

FIGURE 4.6

The Rake palette.

▼ **Brush Scale** increases or decreases the spacing of bristles and affects stroke size.

▼ **Turn Amount** smooths (higher value) or roughens (lower value) curves painted with a rake brush.

▼ **Spread Bristles** joins at the beginning or end of a stroke bristles that have been spread. Deselect this pressure-sensitive option to have bristles run parallel to each other.

▼ **S o f t e n B r i s t l e E d g e** softens the bristles on the edge

of a brush, making them more translucent.

WELL, WELL, WELL

The Well palette, shown in Figure 4.7, adjusts the amount of paint held on a brush, and the way it interacts when it builds up.

▼ Increase your **Resaturation** value to make the color last longer through a stroke.

FIGURE 4.7

The Well palette.

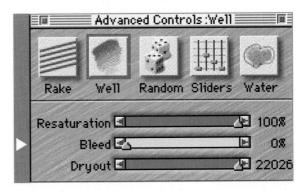

▼ Increase your **Bleed** value to make colors blend more as they build up.

▼ Increase your **Dryout** if you want your medium to stay on your brush longer. A value of 100% results in no dryout. Decreasing this value makes the brush dry out more quickly.

RANDOM ACTS

 The settings on the Random palette contribute to the haphazard nature of a brush stroke, paper texture, or clone.

▼ **Dab Location** refers to the pattern of brush "dabs" that form a brush stroke, for example, the bristle pattern of a bristle brush. Increasing the value increases the randomness of the dabs and ultimately gives you Seurat-like results.

▼ **Clone Location** controls factors associated with cloning methods. Increasing the **Variability** softens brush strokes and makes them less precise. Decreasing **How Often** generates rougher strokes.

▼ **Random Brush Stroke Grain** randomizes paper grain texture and gives you an unrepeating version of the paper grain.

▼ **Random Clone Source** randomizes location and source image parts for a wildly distorted effect.

Still not enough for you? Well, we still have one more trick left up our sleeves—the options on the Expression Sliders palette.

EXPRESSION SLIDERS

The Sliders palette, shown in Figure 4.8, controls how your brushes interact with paper texture, color density, and stroke width. Many of the settings enable mouse users to achieve the effect of using a pressure-sensitive stylus; others are useful for special effects.

▼ **Size** controls how Painter determines brush size.

▼ **Jitter** increases or decreases the randomness of a brush stroke.

▼ **Opacity** determines how Buildup method brushes operate.

▼ **Grain** controls how paper texture is shown through a brush stroke.

▼ **Color** allows you to have two-color brush strokes. Choose one of these settings to determine when each color is used.

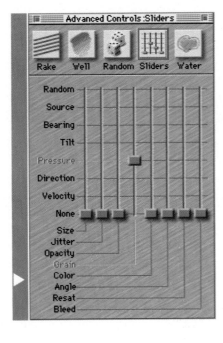

FIGURE 4.8

The Expression Sliders palette.

stylus pressure, stylus direction, stylus velocity (speed), or none (the stroke is unaffected).

WATER COLOR VALUES

The values on the Water palette, shown in Figure 4.9, affect Water Color (Wet method) brushes.

▼ Increasing **Diffusion** increases the feathering strokes on the Wet Paint layer.

49

▼ **Angle** adjusts the direction of dabs in a stroke.

▼ **Resaturation** controls how much color is retained on a brush though a stroke.

▼ **Bleed** determines how colors mix together when you are using a Buildup method brush.

Each of these settings lets you select how you want Painter to determine the options: randomly, according to the source document, bearing and tilt (for tablets that support these features),

▼ Increasing **Wet Fringe** increases the amount of pooling on the Wet Paint layer.

Well, that's it for the basic techniques for customizing brush behavior. Even if you never use them, you'll still have an exceptional supply of default tools to work with. If you're a real adventurer, you'll come up with tons of new variants with which to impress your friends and colleagues. Before you go off and design a slew of new and exciting tools, let's look at how Painter lets you preview new brush strokes and save the ones you really want to keep.

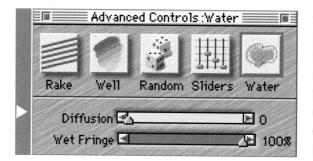

FIGURE 4.9

The Water palette.

tool that makes all of the technical customization we just covered very easy to swallow. Basically, it means you don't have to memorize (or even totally understand) what every customization option is for. Just check it out in the Brush Look Designer, and keep fiddling with it until you see the result you want. (Sorry, but if we told you this earlier, you wouldn't have even read any of the other stuff.)

VIEWING AND SAVING BRUSHES

Painter provides you with the Brush Look Designer palette, a wonderful interactive preview tool to view your brush strokes as you create or edit them. Then you can use the Brush Looks icon on the Brush Controls palette to keep a visual record and library of your brush strokes. Finally, you can add your new custom brushes and variants to the Brushes palette.

THE BRUSH LOOK DESIGNER

The basic purpose of the Brush Look Designer palette is so you can see—as you're working—how custom brush and stroke characteristics will look, right down to the colors you want to use them in.

The Brush Look Designer is *very* easy to use and is an incredibly useful

First, open the palette by selecting **Brush Look Designer** from the **Brushes** cascading menu on the Tools menu. The palette shown in Figure 4.10 is displayed.

You should be looking at a sample brush stroke on a sample background. To change the shape of the sample stroke, simply paint another stroke with your mouse or stylus. To change the stroke color or background, select a color from the primary or secondary color rectangles (respectively) on the Colors palette, then click **Set Colors** on the Brush Look Designer palette.

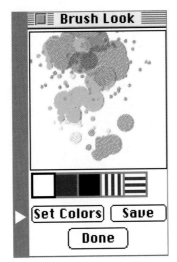

FIGURE 4.10

The Brush Look Designer palette.

Let's try it: Click on the **Save** button and you'll see the Name Brush Look dialog box shown in Figure 4.11.

Enter a name in the Save As field, and click **OK**. That's it! Your new custom brush is saved on the Brush Controls: Look palette.

BRUSH LOOKS

"Okay," you may be saying. "I've just saved my new brush stroke on the Looks palette, but what the heck is that?"

A good way to get a feel for how this works is to select existing default variants from the Brushes palette and see how they look in the Brush Look Designer. Then experiment with them using the customization methods we just discussed. Don't worry—you won't permanently affect your default brushes; unless you save them, your brushes will revert to their original settings.

So what if you come up with a brush you really like? Use it to paint with right away or save it. You can save it as a variant in the Brushes palette or save it on the Looks palette right from the Brush Look Designer.

Simple. It's a visual library of changes you made to a brush stroke using any of the customization methods (including the Papers palette, discussed in the next chapter). **Looks** also memorize and link the paper texture used—unlike saving a brush variant Open the palette by selecting the **Looks** icon.

This palette, shown in Figure 4.12, is already chock full of options that are

FIGURE 4.11

The Name Brush Look dialog box

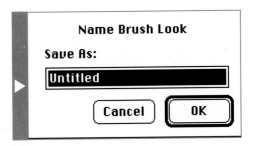

FIGURE 4.12

The Brush Look palette with the Library drawer open.

found under the **Tools** menu. Figure 4.13 displays your options.

SAVING NEW BRUSHES

It's also easy to create a whole new brush category. Of course, you'll want to create a picture to appear alongside the existing pictures on the Brushes palette, so do that first (or you can use any picture that can be imported into Painter). Use the **Rectangular Selection** tool to choose a square portion of the image to be used. Then select **Save Brush** from the cascading menu, enter a name for your brush, and click **OK**. Your new brush and its mug shot are now the last option on the Brushes palette. Now, create as many new variants for your brush as you like.

ready to use. Use this palette the same way you use the Brushes palette: Scroll through the colorful icons, and click to select one.

Click on **Library...** to access a slew of additional brush libraries available from Fractal Design Corp. If you ordered the Trees and Leaves Library package (see Appendix C), you will already have two additional libraries.

SAVING BRUSHES AND VARIANTS

You also have the option of saving a custom brush directly to the Brushes palette. To see your choices for saving and deleting brushes and variants, select the cascading **Brushes** menu

SAVING AND DELETING VARIANTS

To save a brush stroke as a new variant of the currently selected brush, select **Save Variant...** from the cascading menu. Then enter a brush name in the **Save As** field of the Save Variant dialog box. Click **OK**, and it's saved.

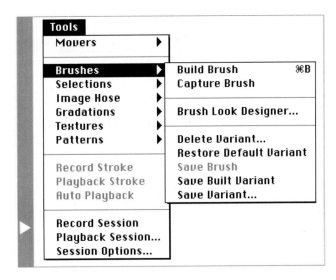

FIGURE 4.13

*The cascading **Brushes** menu.*

To permanently change an existing variant, select the variant, and apply whatever customization you like. Then select **Save Built Variant** from the cascading menu. If you change an existing variant and later decide you liked the original better, simply select **Restore Default Variant** to bring back the original one.

To permanently erase a variant, select the variant you want to delete on the Brushes palette. Then choose **Delete Variant...** from the cascading menu. Painter asks you again if you really want to delete the variant. If you do, click **Yes** to complete the action. If not, click **No** to cancel it.

Remember, if you don't save either to the Brushes palette or the Brush Look palette, your changes disappear as soon as you select another brush or variant. So be sure to save the effects you'd like to use again.

CUSTOM BRUSH SHAPES

Use the **Capture Brush** option to save custom brush shapes. You can capture anything, from footprints to smiley faces. Draw your shape, select it with the **Rectangular Selection** tool, and select **Capture Brush**. Adjust the nib on the Size palette (Brush Controls), and click **Build**. If you want to keep this new brush, save it as described previously.

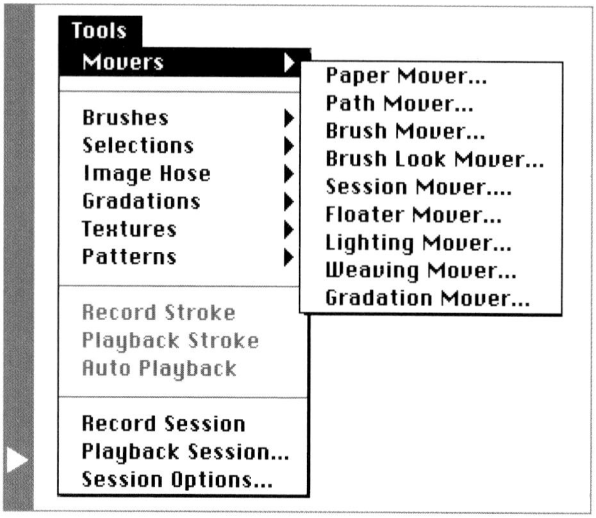

FIGURE 4.14

The cascading **Movers** *menu.*

CUSTOM BRUSHES AND BRUSH LOOK PALETTES

It's easy to set up custom Brushes palettes or Brush Look palettes for individual clients or projects. Select either **Brush Mover...** or **Brush Look**

Mover... from the cascading **Mover** menu (under the Tools menu), as shown in Figure 4.14.

Depending on your selection, you'll now see either the Brush Mover or Brush Look Mover dialog box. Except for the title, they look and operate

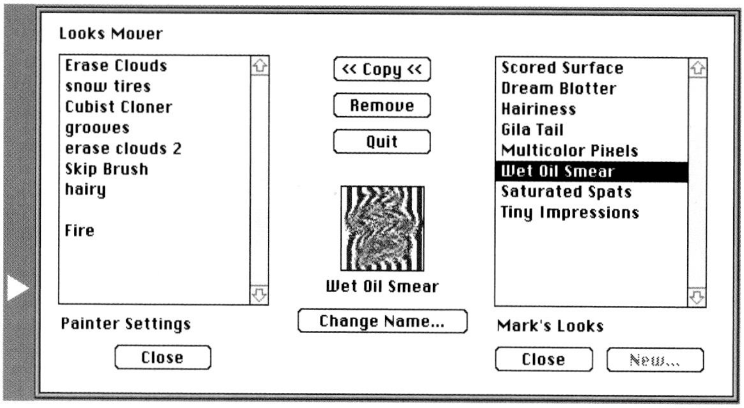

FIGURE 4.15

The Brush Look Mover dialog box.

alike. Let's use the Brush Looks Mover, shown in Figure 4.15, as our example.

Use this dialog box to move brushes into your new library (**>>Copy>>**), remove brushes from an existing library (**Remove**), close an open library (**Close**), open an existing library (**Open**), or create a new library (**New...**). Simply select the brush or library you wish to use, close, or change, then click on the button that performs the action. When you're done, click on **Quit** to close the dialog box.

WHEW!

We've finally covered all of the brush customization options available in Painter. If you can think of anything that Fractal Design left out, call them up—I'm sure they'd love to hear about it. But if you're like us, your head is probably spinning from all of the choices already available, so take a few minutes to go for a walk or splash cold water on your face before moving on to the next chapter.

PRACTICE SESSION

1. Open a new file, choosing black for the background. Select the **Impressionist Artists** brush from the Brushes palette. Change the Subcategory **Method** to **Hard Drip**. Choose a multicolored brown from the Impressionist color page on the Colors palette. Now draw the wood for a campfire.

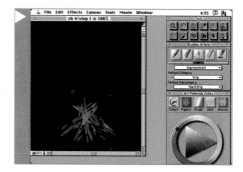

2. On the Brushes palette, select the **Coarse Smeary Bristles** variant of the **Liquid** brush using the Controls palette, reduce the **Grain** to **50%**, and increase the **Opacity** to **85%**. Change the **Method Subcategory** to **Grainy Drip**. Next, paint on some red, orange, and yellow, applying darker colors toward the source of the fire. We've selected our colors from the Hi Key color set.

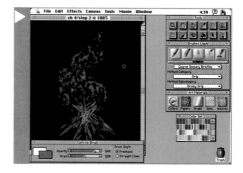

3. To get instant fire, just add liquid: Select the **Distorto Liquid** tool, open the Size palette, and decrease the Size slider to about **20**. Click **Build**, then smear your fire upward.

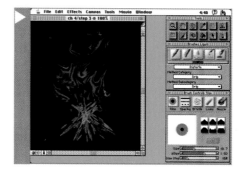

Color

CHAPTER 5

Colors are our perception of different wavelengths of light. Almost all colors can be created by using one of three color-mixing systems, each of which is best suited for a different purpose.

▼ **RGB** is typically used to create transmitted colors, and is the method used by color monitors and color televisions. RGB shows colors by using clusters of red, green, and blue phosphors, often referred to as *pixels*.

▼ **HSV** relates to the way the human eye perceives color. HSV stands for hue, saturation, and value (often called *brightness*). Hue refers to the property of a particular color relating to its frequency, or wavelength, of light. *Saturation* is the extent to which a color is comprised of a selected hue, rather than a combination of hue and white, as in the difference between red (a heavily saturated color) and pink (a less saturated color). *Value* is the degree of lightness or darkness in a color. Painter uses HSV on its Color palette because this color-wheel based system is most familiar to artists.

▼ **CMYK** is best suited for representing reflected colors—for printing colors. Generally used for producing printing plates for four-color process printing, CMYK is a color model using cyan, magenta, yellow, and black inks for different colors. Painter *does not* support the CMYK format and will neither save (except as an EPS DCS file format that can't be reopened by Painter) to it nor import files in this format.

Remember, Painter mixes paint on the Color palette using HSV and saves files in RGB format. It *does not* use CMYK. If you are planning to import your files into a page layout program or output RC paper or film for four-color process printing, you must save your Painter files as EPS DCS files, which are CMYK. This format is discussed in Chapter 1.

MORE USES FOR THE COLORS PALETTE

 The basic operation of the Colors icon on the Art Materials palette is covered in Chapter 3. This section discusses some more advanced uses for that palette. To access all of the options for the Colors icon, click on the zoom button on the upper right of the palette's title bar. The expanded palette is shown in Figure 5.1.

58

PRIMARY AND SECONDARY COLORS

Depending on the brush you choose, your strokes can comprise a primary color, a secondary color, and the range of colors between them.

Click on the front rectangle on the lower left of the Colors palette to select your primary painting color, and on the back rectangle to select your secondary painting color. Figure 5.2 shows blue chosen as the primary color (front rectangle) and red (back rectangle) as the secondary color.

The use of primary and secondary colors is controlled by the Sliders icon on the Advanced Controls palette. When the color slider is set to **None,** you can only paint using one color at a

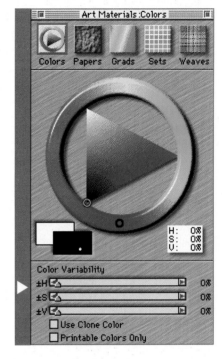

FIGURE 5.1

The expanded Colors icon section of the Art Materials palette.

59

FIGURE 5.2

The Color palette with blue selected as a primary color and red selected as a secondary color.

time. Any of the other selections allows you to paint in two colors and determine when the primary color is used and when the secondary color is added.

PAINTING WITH MULTIPLE COLORS

You can also set up your Color palette to paint using more than two colors by using the **±HSV Color Variability** sliders on the bottom of the extended Color palette.

▼ Increase the **±H** (hue) percentage to increase the number of hues in a brush stroke.

▼ Increase the **±S** (saturation) percentage to increase the number of saturations in a brush stroke.

▼ Increase the **±V** (value) percentage to increase the limit of luminances in a brush stroke.

Your kaleidoscopic selection is previewed in the front rectangle, as in Figure 5.3. Figure 5.4 shows some multicolored brush strokes.

PRINTABLE COLORS

Although you have a palette of 16 million colors to paint with, an offset printing press can't always print every color you come up with. To remedy this, click in the **Printable Colors Only** check box (on the bottom of the palette) to select it. If you have not selected a printable color, the on-screen color remains the same but the printable color is displayed in the color rectangle on the palette. The colors you paint with will now be the printable colors displayed in the rectangles, not the on-screen colors.

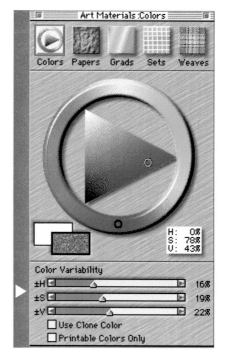

FIGURE 5.3

Selecting a multicolored brush stroke.

FIGURE 5.4

Multicolored brush strokes.

You may also apply printable colors to a selected area of an image by selecting the area *before* selecting **Printable Colors...**.

CLONING COLORS

You may also clone, or copy, a color or portion of colors from one painting to another, or even within the same painting.

Oops! I Forgot to Check the Box

You've just spent three weeks creating the masterpiece of your lifetime and are ready to send it to your printer. Oh, no! You forgot to check **Printable Colors**, and you have no idea how your piece will print. Not to worry— you can change your 16 million colors to printable colors at any time in a project (although it's always best to do it before you start working).

Open the Effects menu and select **Printable Colors...** from the **Tonal Control** cascading menu. Click **OK** in the dialog box shown in Figure 5.5, and it's done.

Click on the **Use Clone Color** check box on the Color palette. Then select one of the variants of the **Cloner** brush on the Brushes palette (see Chapter 8 for more details on cloning brushes). Click once in the source area.

61

FIGURE 5.5

The Printable Colors dialog box with a preview.

Then, while holding down the **Control** key, click and drag over the area you want to paint. Your source image re-creates itself using the variant you selected, as in Figure 5.6.

COLOR FOR VIDEO

As with offset printing presses, not all colors displayed on your monitor can be used in video. However, most colors on your monitor will be video legal (except bright yellows and cyan blues).

Open the Effects menu and select **Video Legal Colors...** from the **Tonal Control** cascading menu. You'll see a preview of the video-legal image in the dialog box shown in Figure 5.7. Select either the **NTSC** (United States) or **PAL** (European) video system from the pop-up menu, click **OK**, and it's done.

You may also apply video-legal colors to a selected area of an image by selecting the area before selecting **Video Legal Colors**.

THE FILL TOOL

The Fill tool is great for dumping color into an image, a selected mask, or a cartoon cel.

To use it, select the **Fill tool**. Select the type of area you want to fill from the Controls palette by clicking once on the appropriate radio button. Then click the tool on the image, selection, mask, or cartoon cel you want to fill.

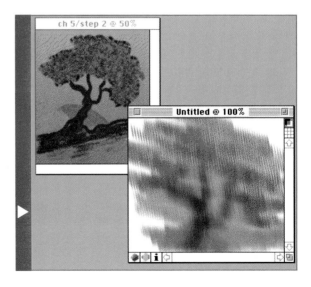

FIGURE 5.6 ▶

*A source image (left), and its cloned colors using the **Driving Rain Cloner** variant.*

62

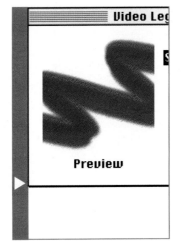

FIGURE 5.7

The Video Legal dialog box with a preview of the image.

GRADIENT FILLS

To fill an area with a gradation, click on the **Grads** icon on the Art Materials palette.

Open the Gradients drawer, shown in Figure 5.9, and you'll see a library of preset gradients (also known as a *color ramp*) from which you can choose (click on the icon to choose a gradient). You may open and save gradation libraries using the **Library** button as you would any other Painter library. Close the drawer to access controls you can use to change existing gradients or create your own.

When you select a gradient icon, it is displayed in the large preview square on the lower left of the palette. Click on this square, shown in Figure 5.10, and the gradient rotates. The gradient continues to rotate until you stop it by selecting an angle by clicking in the ring around it. (It looks pretty neat, but don't let it rotate too long, some of these can hypnotize you or give you

You also have some options as to the type of fill to use:

▼ **Current Color** fills an area with the flat tone selected as your primary color on the Colors palette.

▼ **Gradation** fills an area with a gradient fill, from primary color to secondary color.

▼ **Clone Source** fills an area with a selected part of another image—a "clone source" (see Chapter 8 for more details on cloning images).

Weaving fills an area with a weaving pattern.

FIGURE 5.8

The Controls palette for the **Fill** *tool.*

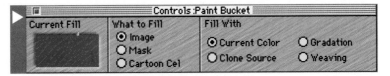

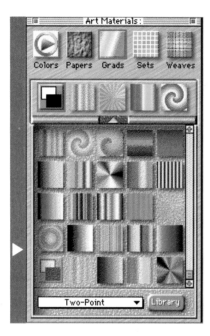

FIGURE 5.9

The Art Materials:Grads palette with the library drawer open.

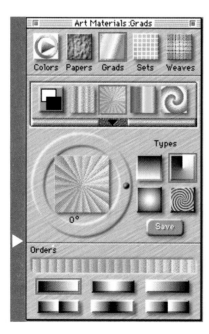

FIGURE 5.10

Changing a gradient on the Art Materials:Grads palette.

motion sickness.) You may also select an angle by clicking in the angle ring or dragging the red dot around the ring to specify an angle in 1-degree increments.

The gradient icon with the black and white squares on it allows you to apply a gradient fill that uses the currently selected primary and secondary colors.

You may also use the **Types** icons to change the style of gradation shown in the preview square. To save a gradient you have changed or created, click **Save**, enter a name for the gradient, and click **OK**. If you are using the currently selected colors in a gradient, the icon retains those colors, but it always applies the currently selected colors. Holding down the **Command** key while dragging the red ball changes the radius of a spiral gradient fill.

Click on the zoom box to see the options on the extended palette. These icons control the placement of color in the gradient.

To capture a gradation from an image and place it in your library, select the gradation using the **Rectangular Selection** tool. Select the **Capture Gradation** option from the cascading **Gradations** menu on the Tools menu. Name your gradation, click **OK**, and it is added to the current library.

WEAVING FILLS

Weaving fills places woven pattern in an area. To use it, click on the **Weaving** icon on the Art Materials palette.

Open the Weaving drawer, shown in Figure 5.11, and you'll see a library of preset weaves from which you can choose (click on the icon to choose a gradient). You may open and

save weaving libraries using the **Library** button as you would any other Painter library. Close the drawer to access controls you can use to change existing weaves or create your own.

When you select a gradient icon, it is displayed in the large preview square on the lower left of the palette, shown in Figure 5.12. Click on the **Fiber Type** preview box to change the fiber type: two-dimensional or three-dimensional complete with shadows (this won't always be reflected in the preview square).

Use the sliders on the extended palette (click the zoom box to open it) to change the scaling (space between

FIGURE 5.11

The Art Materials:Weaves palette with the library drawer open.

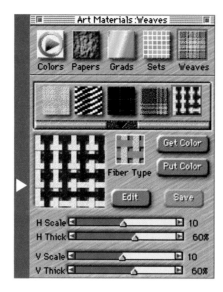

FIGURE 5.12

Changing the settings on the extended Art Materials:Weaves palette.

the **Edit** button to change specific Warp and Weft settings. This dialog box uses Fractal Design Corporation's own weaving language, explained in Technical Note #4 found on the Painter Extras CD-ROM. You may also call their technical support staff for help with this.

The **Save** and **Library** buttons for weavings work just like the buttons on the Grads palette.

them) and thickness of the threads. You have separate controls for vertical and horizontal threads.

Changing the Colors on a Weave

Click on **Get Color** to open the color set for a currently selected weave. To change these colors, select a new color from the Colors palette. Hold down the **Option** key and click on the color in the color set you want to replace. Go back to the Weaves palette, click on **Put Color**, and the old color is replaced with the new one.

If you really know what you are doing when it comes to weaving, use

CARTOON CEL FILLS

Cartoon cel fills allow you to fill an area enclosed by line art. You must draw your outlines with the **Scratchboard** tool, in black, for this feature to work.

Choose **Auto Mask** from the cascading Mask menu on the Edit menu. Select **Image Luminance** from the pop-up menu, and click **OK**. This creates a mask protecting your outlines.

Select the **Fill** tool, and check the **Cartoon Cel** radio button on the

FIGURE 5.13 ▶

A *cartoon cel fill.*

Controls palette. Use the **Fill** tool and the Colors palette to add colors inside your outlines.

Figure 5.13 shows a cartoon cel fill.

If you are drawing outlines that are not completely closed, the color will leak out. To avoid this, turn on the mask and use any masking brush to plug the leak (if you do not know how to do this, please see Chapter 7).

LOCKOUT COLOR AND MASK THRESHOLD

Lockout color prevents a particular color from being painted over.

On the Colors palette, select the color you want to lock out. Double-click on the **Fill** tool icon to open the Lockout Color dialog box. Click on **Set** (this automatically selects the checkbox and updates the preview square). The

default setting for this feature is black, to work with Cartoon Cel fills.

If you would like to protect nonblack lines, use the **Mask Threshold** slider. There is no set formula for making this work, so you'll have to play with it a bit.

When you have locked out your color or adjusted the masking threshold, click **OK** to accept your changes.

COLOR SETS

 To open an existing color set, select the **Sets** icons from the Art Materials palette. Click the **Library** button, select the set you want to open (make sure you are in the **Colors, Weaves, and Grads** folder in the Painter 3 application folder), and click **OK**. Figure 5.14 shows the Pantone color set with the Sets palette.

You can create a new color set based on the colors in an existing image. Click the **New Set** button, and an empty set is created. Make sure the image is open, and using the **Dropper** tool, select a color to add to the set. Click the **Add Color** button. Use the **Dropper** and the **Add Color** button this

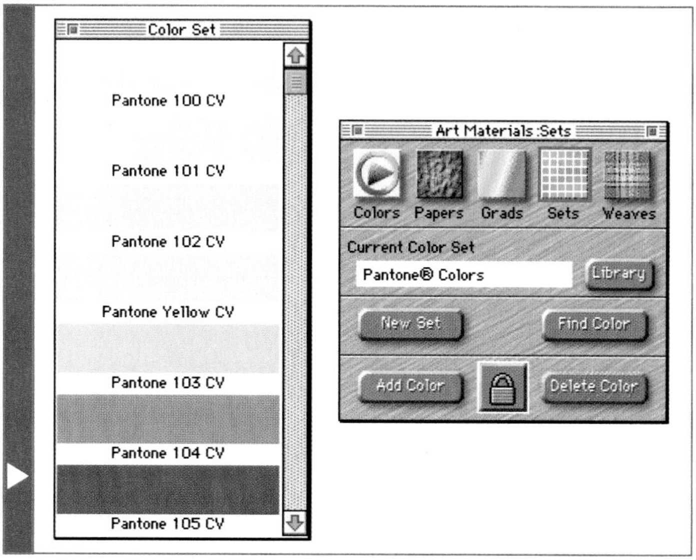

FIGURE 5.14

The Pantone color set and the Sets palette.

way for each color you want to add to the set. **Delete Color** removes a selected color. If you would like to name the colors in a set, double click on the color, enter a name, and click **OK**. When you are done, click on the close box (on the upper left of the Sets window), and follow the prompts to name the set.

These controls may also be used to edit existing color sets.

The **Find Color** button lets you search a set (by name) for a particular color).

The options on the extended palette, shown in Figure 5.15, allow you to customize the way your sets are displayed.

The **Color Square Size** options reduce and increase the width and height of the squares. Check **Display Text** to have color names displayed below each color square.

The **Color Set Size** controls change the width and height of the set window. Check **Display Grid** to place a thin line between color squares.

ANNOTATING COLORS

The Annotation feature labels colors in your image (even on floaters) based on the names in a color set. Annotations "float" over your image and can be saved in files using Painter's native RIFF format.

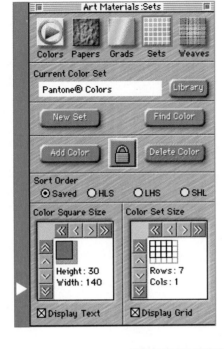

FIGURE 5.15

The extended Sets palette.

Release the cursor, and the annotated name is displayed. Continue annotating colors in this manner.

To delete an annotation, select its label and press **Delete**.

When you have completed your annotations, click the **Done** button.

Figure 5.16 shows an image being annotated.

Make sure the View Annotations option on the Canvas menu is selected. Select **Annotate...** from the Canvas menu. Click on the color you want to annotate. A dialog box with a Done button is displayed. Ignore it for now, and drag your cursor off the color.

FIGURE 5.16

Annotating the colors in an image.

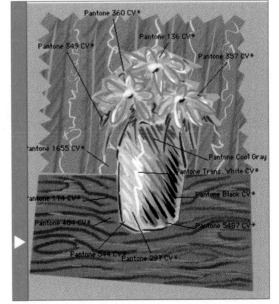

PRACTICE SESSION

1. Open a new file (Painter's default size is just fine). On the Colors palette, select a light blue as the primary color (front rectangle) and a brown as the secondary color (back rectangle). Select the **Fill** tool.

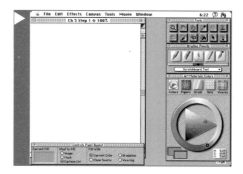

2. Open the Grads palette and from the library drawer, select the black and white **Two-Point** icon. Close the drawer. Use the red ball to set the ramp angle at 90°. Select the **Image** radio button on the Controls palette, and click in your image to fill it with the gradation.

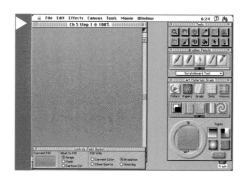

3. On the Colors palette, use the color triangle and the **±HSV** sliders to create some multicolored strokes. Use those color strokes with the Chalk brushes to sketch out a little landscape using multicolored strokes. Notice that with a combination of the texture-sensitive pastels and the multicolored strokes, you'll only need to make about four selections from the Color palette to sketch out this little landscape.

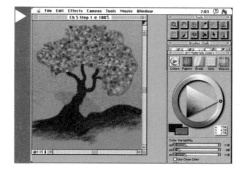

Scratching the Surface

PAPER TEXTURE AND SURFACE CONTROL

CHAPTER 6

One of the best features in Painter—there are so many of them—is the ability to have your tools interact with a plethora of surface textures. It's one thing to be able to paint electronically with realistic brushes. It's amazing to be able to do this on a vast assortment of canvases and other surfaces and to see your tools interacting with these surfaces. After reading this chapter, you'll also be able to apply special effects to your painting surfaces, from marbling and distorting images to adjusting tones and adding light sources.

TEXTURES: THE PAPERS PALETTE

 Opening the Papers palette (on the Art Materials palette) is a sensual experience. Really. You can almost feel your brushes interacting with whatever paper grain you have selected.

When you select a paper grain by clicking on its icon, you won't see the background of your image change to that texture. Instead, you'll see the texture reflected in your brush strokes, if you are using a paper-texture sensitive tool. (Any brush that uses a **Grainy Method** reacts to paper texture.) Figure 6.1 shows the **Chalk** brush being used with a variety of textures available on the default Papers palette.

Use the zoom box to expand the palette. You can increase the size of the paper grain by increasing the value on the **Scale** slider. Check the **Invert Grain** check box (three guesses as to what this one does) to invert the grain of your paper. **Random Grain** (on the Advanced Controls:Random palette) randomizes the texture and gives you an unrepeating version of a texture.

To access an even cooler assortment of textures, open the Library drawer, click on the **Library** button,

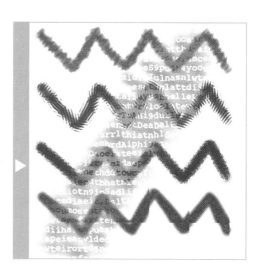

FIGURE 6.1 ▶

Using the **Chalk** *brush with the default Paper palette library.*

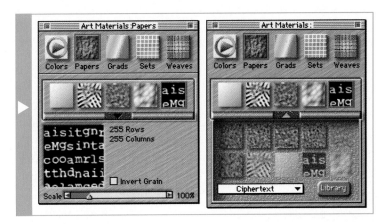

FIGURE 6.2

The extended Papers palette with the Library drawer closed (left) and open (right).

asshown in figure 6.2, and select from additional texture files: **More Paper Textures**, **Simple Patterns**, **Texture Sample**, **Wild Textures**, and **More Wild Textures** (your default file is **Paper Textures**).

APPLYING PAPER GRAIN TO AN ENTIRE IMAGE

In addition to applying grain to individual strokes, you can apply a three-dimensional paper grain to an entire image. This works before, during, or after adding brush strokes to an image.

Using the Papers palette, select the grain and other options you want to apply. Then open the Effects menu and select **Apply Surface Texture...** from the **Surface Control** cascading menu. The Apply Surface Texture dialog box, shown in Figure 6.3, gives you a preview of how your image will look with the selected texture. (If you have a slower computer, please be patient while this dialog box makes its appearance.)

73

FIGURE 6.3

The Apply Surface Texture dialog box.

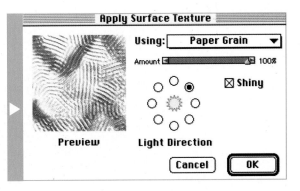

Make sure **Paper Grain** is chosen on the **Using** pop-up menu, adjust the **Amount** slider to the percentage of grain you want to apply, and click **OK**. Voila! Instant texture.

If you choose **Image Luminance** in the **Using** pop-up menu, Painter uses the brightness of an image to decide where to place texture.

Reserve some time for either of these options to process.

APPLYING COLOR AND PAPER GRAIN

Use the **Color Overlay...** feature, also found under the **Surface Control** cascading menu, to add both color and texture at the same time to either an entire image or a selected portion.

In the Color Overlay dialog box, (Figure 6.4), select a model: **Dye Concentration** allows color to be absorbed by the paper, **Hiding Power**

allows the color to cover an underlying image.

Adjust the **Opacity** slider until you see the results you want in the **Preview** window. Next, select a mode from the **Using** pop-up menu:

▼ **Uniform Color** overlays a flat, untextured tint.

▼ **Paper Grain** overlays a texture selected in the Papers palette. (You may switch to the open Papers palette from this dialog box.)

▼ **Mask** adds texture around a mask (see Chapter 7 for more information on masks).

▼ **Image Luminance** generates a texture based on the brightness of an image.

▼ **Original Luminance** texturizes a cloned image based on the bright-

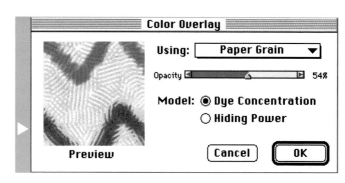

FIGURE 6.4

The Color Overlay dialog box.

74

ness of a source image (see Chapter 8 for more information on cloning).

When the **Preview** box shows the results you want to achieve, click **OK**.

CREATING AND EDITING PAPER TEXTURES

If that's not enough for you (boy, are you demanding), you can create your own paper textures and libraries, or edit existing ones.

Repeating Textures

Use the **Make Paper Texture** choice on the **Textures** cascading option on the Tools menu to make custom surfaces from a selection of preset patterns. From the Repeating Texture dialog box, shown in Figure 6.5, make any of the following adjustments:

▼ Select a pattern type from the **Pattern** pop-up menu (**Halftone, New Halftone, Line, Diamond, Square, Circle, Ellipse,** or **Triangle**).

▼ Increase the value on the **Spacing** slider to increase the space between each pattern element.

▼ Change the value on the **Angle** slider to change the angle of the pattern.

Your changes are displayed in the **Preview** window. When you achieve the results you want, name the pattern and click **OK**, and it is added to the end of the open paper texture library.

Capturing a Texture

Let's say you've created a brush stroke or a series of strokes that you want to use as an underlying texture for a

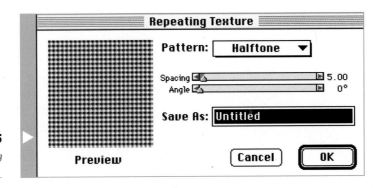

FIGURE 6.5

The Repeating Texture dialog box.

series of digital paintings the Metropolitan Museum of Art has commissioned you to paint. Well, Painter makes it even easier than you would have thought to use that texture again and again.

Simply select the area (using the **Rectangular Selection** tool) you want to add to a library and choose **Capture Texture...** from the **Textures** cascading menu. Use the **Crossfade** slider to indicate how much the selected area repeats in the texture, enter a texture name, and click **OK**. Your texture is now added to the end of the open paper texture library.

SURFACE CONTROL

The section on texture talked about applying grains and textures to the surface of an image. *Surface control* refers to other types of effects that can be applied to the surface of an image, such as adjusting tone, distorting an image, applying a light source, and adding other special effects.

TONAL CONTROL

Did your mother ever tell you to change your tone?

Well, here's your chance to make Mom real happy.

Under the Effects menu you will find the **Tonal Control** cascading menu. You have several options here that we haven't covered yet. All of these options can be applied to an entire image or a selected or masked part.

▼ **Adjust Colors** lets you calibrate the HSV values of an image.

▼ **Adjust Selected Colors** adjusts HSV values based on a central color (selected by clicking in the image).

▼ **Brightness/Contrast** adjusts the brightness and contrast from the dialog box shown in Figure 6.6.

▼ **Equalize** balances the brightness and contrast settings to optimize them. It finds the lightest and darkest values in an image, averages them, and redistributes the values in between.

FIGURE 6.6

The Brightness/Contrast dialog box.

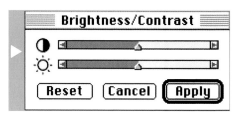

Use the black and white triangle sliders under the histogram (the black mountain-like image) to adjust your image. Adjust the **Brightness** slider to increase or decrease gamma (midtone values—everything but black and white). You'll see the changes on-screen as you move the sliders. Click on **Apply** if you want to keep your changes. (Huh?) Forget all of that, just look at Figure 6.7 to see what it does.

▼ **Posterize** reduces the amount of colors (or grayscales) in an image. Simply enter the number of colors you want your image reduced to in the Posterize dialog box and click **OK**. Figure 6.8 shows an image before and after posterization.

▼ **Negative** turns your image into a negative, as in Figure 6.9.

ORIENTATION AND DISTORTION

These options are great for getting Picasso-like results. Under the Effects menu is the **Orientation** cascading menu, which allows you access to the following manipulations:

▼ **Rotate** turns your image (or selected area) in increments of .1 degrees. Enter the value in the dialog box, and click **OK**.

▼ **Scale** changes the dimensions of the image or selected area. Either click and drag on the handles that appear around the image or enter horizontal and vertical scale values

77

FIGURE 6.7 ▶

An image before (left) and after (right) equalization. **Dock with Colorful Boats** *painting courtesy of Dennis Orlando.*

FIGURE 6.8

An image before (left) and after (right) posterization.

in the dialog box. Click **Constrain Aspect Ratio** to proportionally scale an image. Click **OK** to accept your changes.

 Distort warps the image in a selected area. Click and drag on the handles that appear around the selection. If you click on the **Better** check box, you get a more accurate distortion, but it takes much longer to render. Click **OK** to keep your changes.

FIGURE 6.9

An image before (left) and after (right) using the **Negative** *option.*

▼ **Flip Horizontal** works on an entire image or a selected area.

▼ **Flip Vertical** works on an entire image or a selected area.

DYE CONCENTRATION

Dye concentration adjusts the intensity of color in all or a selected part of an image. The Adjust Dye Concentration dialog box, shown in Figure 6.10, is another place you can add texture to an image. Access this dialog box from the **Surface Control** cascading menu under the Effects menu.

Select from the following options in the **Using** pop-up menu:

▼ **Uniform Adjustment** adjusts color. It does not add texture.

▼ **Paper Grain** adjusts color while adding a texture selected from the open Paper palette.

▼ **Mask** adds texture around a mask (see Chapter 7 for more information on masks).

▼ **Image Luminance** generates a texture based on the brightness of an image.

▼ **Original Luminance** texturizes a cloned image based on the brightness of a source image (see Chapter 8 for more information on cloning).

Use the **Maximum** and **Minimum** sliders to adjust the intensity of color in an image. When the **Preview** box reflects the results you want, click **OK** to accept the changes.

79

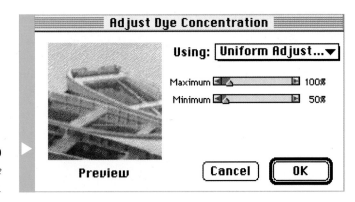

FIGURE 6.10

The Adjust Dye Concentration dialog box.

LIGHTING

Use this feature, also found under the **Surface Control** cascading menu, to add one or more light sources to all or a selected part of an image. You can even select the color of the light source.

This option is only available to users working on a computer with a floating-point unit (math coprocessor). If you do not have a floating-point unit built into your computer, this option is grayed out.

Use the scrolling palette in the bottom left of the Apply Lighting dialog box to select the type of lighting you want to apply.

To edit the light source, adjust the sliders until the results you want are displayed in the Preview box.

To add color to the light source, click in the **Light Color** square. Select a color from the color picker, and click **OK**. Use the same process to select an **Ambient Light Color** (the surrounding light).

If you've edited an existing light source and would like to save it, click on the **Save** button, enter a name for your new lighting, and click on **OK**. Your new lighting is now added to the scrolling palette.

When your lighting is absolutely perfect, click **OK** to accept the changes. Please be aware that, although it's a really neat feature, this is one of the slowest options in Painter (unless you are using a DSP-equipped AV or a PowerMac). You may want to use it just before a lunch break. If you are lucky, it may be ready in time for dinner.

FOCUS

The options on the **Focus** cascading menu allow you to sharpen and blur your image or a selected portion of it.

▼ **Sharpen** increases contrast of adjacent pixels to increase the clarity of an image. Be careful with this one; you can get some really wild results if you oversharpen. Figure 6.11 shows the sharpening of an image.

▼ **Soften** is the opposite of **Sharpen**, and has the same effect as putting a filter on a photographic lens, as in Figure 6.12.

▼ **Motion Blur** creates the illusion of movement by making an image appear as if you had photographed it while it was moving, as in Figure 6.13.

80

FIGURE 6.11 ▶

An image before and after sharpening.

▼ **Glass Distortion** makes your image appear as though you were viewing it through glass, as in Figure 6.14.

OTHER SURFACE EFFECTS

Now we're getting into an even wilder set of tools found on the **Esoterica** cascading menu (under the Effects menu).

81

FIGURE 6.12 ▶

Softening an image.

FIGURE 6.13 ▶

Using **Motion Blur***.*

Marbling

Marbling turns any image (all or a selection) into a marbled masterpiece. Specify the **Rake Path** (direction of marbling) to get the effects you want. Figure 6.15 shows an example.

Blobs

True to its name, **Blobs** uses either a color or an item on the current clipboard to place floating blobs on an image. Blobbed images are great candidates for marbling. Figure 6.16 is blobbed.

FIGURE 6.14 ▶

Using **Glass Distortion***.*

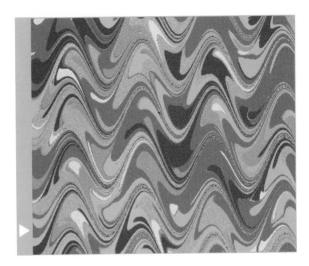

FIGURE 6.15

*Applying **Marbling**.*

This option is only available to users working on a computer with a floating-point unit (math coprocessor). If you do not have a floating-point unit built into your computer, this option is grayed out.

Grid Paper

Grid Paper adds grid lines to all or part of an image. These lines are editable as if they were applied by painting them on.

83

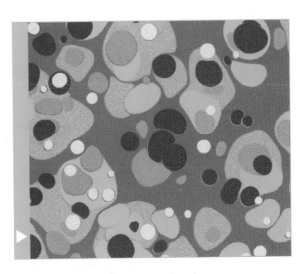

FIGURE 6.16

A blobbed image.

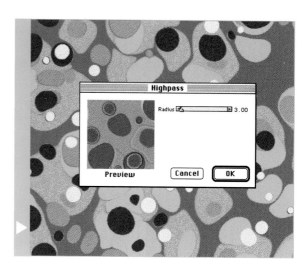

FIGURE 6.17
*Applying **Highpass**.*

Highpass

Highpass lets higher-frequency areas show through while suppressing lower-frequency areas. It has the effect of highlighting areas of brightness and increasing contrast in areas that are lacking contrast, as in Figure 6.17.

PLUGINS

If you chose to access third-party plugins while installing Painter, you can access them through the **Plugin Filter** cascading menu under the Effects menu. If you did not locate any plugins during installation, this option is grayed out.

Enough of this chatter. Let's try some of this stuff.

PRACTICE SESSION

1. Use the **Sharp Pencil** in black to sketch your best friend. Open the Wild Textures library, and select the **Nature Spots** pattern for Spot. Increase the **Scale** to **200%**, choose a medium brown, and using the **Sharp Chalk** brush fill in the dog's coat.

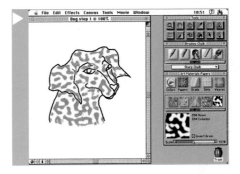

2. Click on the **Invert Grain** checkbox on the extended Papers palette. Select a lighter brown, and fill in the rest of the dog's coat.

3. Using the **Single-Pixel** pen, paint in the details: eyes, nose, and whiskers. Notice no paper grain shows through because this tool doesn't use a Grainy method. Next, apply a background using a variety of textures and colors with the **Chalk** and **Pencil** brushes.

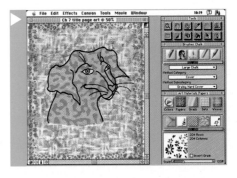

85

Selections, Masks, and Floaters

CHAPTER 7

A selection, also known as a *path*, is used in painter to select an area, to create a mask, and to create a floater.

A *mask* is applied to certain areas of an image to protect them while you work on other areas. F*loaters* are selected or masked areas that are turned into objects that can be moved time and again.

Selections, masks, and floaters are not only handy for selecting and protecting areas of a painting, but also for applying special effects, textures, text, and fills to specific areas of a painting.

SELECTION PATHS

Selection paths are displayed with a moving dotted line, also known as marching ants or a marquee. Selections remain around areas, even if they are not active. In that case, they are displayed as a solid black or red line. There are a few different types of paths in Painter:

▼ **Outline paths** are selections that are inactive, shown with a solid red or black line.

▼ **Curve paths** have solid outlines with control points and handles, like freehand and Bézier curves in many illustration programs. You

may also import curve paths from other applications.

▼ **Mask representation paths** are selections painted right onto the mask layer.

THE PATH LESS TRAVELED

There are a number of tools that can create paths, some on the Tools palette, others on the Brushes palette. Let's take a look at them.

Outline Selection Tool

This tool works like the pen tools in illustration programs. You may use it to draw freehand or Bézier paths. It also has a straight-line mode. After you select this tool, these options become available on the Controls palette. Check the radio button for the mode you want to use.

▼ **Freehand.** Use the **Outline Selection** tool to click and drag across the area you want to select.

▼ **Straight lines.** Click on the origin point of the shape you want to draw, and continue clicking until you close your polygon. If you click and hold, Painter displays a guide showing you where your line segment lays. Holding the **Shift** key while clicking constrains your segments to 45-degree angles. When you have completed your polygon, press **Enter**.

▼ **Bézier.** Click on an origin point, continue holding down your cursor button, and pull out a handle in the direction you want your curve to go. Continue drawing segments in this way. If you don't pull out a handle, that segment will be a straight line. If you make a mistake, use the **Delete** key to remove the most recently drawn segment. Click in the origin point to end your curve. The selection points that appear when you are done can be used to later edit and manipulate this shape.

Text Selection Tool

The **Text Selection** tool creates paths made of type for some incredible effects. After you select this tool, use the Controls palette to select typeface, point size, and tracking. Click in your image, and begin typing. Once placed in your image, text works just like any other selection.

Figure 7.1 shows these tools in action.

FIGURE 7.1 ▶

From top to bottom, a rectangular selection, an oval selection, a freehand selection, a straight-line selection, a Bézier selection, and a text selection.

The Path Adjuster and Controls Palette

 Use the **Path Adjuster** tool to edit selections and control their use. When you select this tool, the Controls palette shown in Figure 7.2 is displayed.

The row of brown **Drawing** buttons (far left) determines how the selection works on your image.

 Turns off the selection.

 Changes the protected areas to inside the selection.

 Changes the protected area to outside the selection (makes "reverse" or "negative" masks).

The row of multicolored **Visibility** buttons determines how you'll view a selection on-screen.

 Makes the selection invisible, but still active according to the selected **Drawing** icon..

 Displays the mask using a flat color. The area covered with the color is the protected area (unless you have selected the reverse selection icon, above).

 Displays the selection using the marching ants outline (dotted line).

These icons can also be accessed from the image window icons on the lower left of every image window, as shown in Figure 7.3.

Click and hold on the brown **Drawing** icon to bring up the top row of selection use icons or on the multicolored **Visibility** icon to bring up the row of display options. The currently selected option for each row is displayed on the image window.

The **Feathering** slider "feathers," or blends, the edges of a mask, as if with an airbrush. Increase the slider value to get the effect shown in Figure 7.4, reduce it to **0** to eliminate the effect.

The feather stays with the mask, even if it is edited or manipulated,

90

FIGURE 7.2

The Controls palette for the **Path** *Adjuster* *tool.*

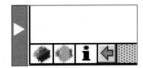

FIGURE 7.3

*The image
window icons.*

unless you select it and change the setting on the palette.

Masking Brushes

Masking brushes give you another option for masking selections using brush strokes.

Masking brushes are available on the Brushes palette:

▼ Grainizer

▼ Big Masking Pen

▼ Masking Airbrush

▼ Masking Chalk

▼ Masking Pen

▼ Single Pixel Masking

Figure 7.5 shows sample strokes from each brush.

You may customize masking brushes using the brush customizing techniques covered in Chapter 4.

EDITING PATHS

Selection paths add a new dimension to your work by allowing you to isolate different areas of a painting. They are also very flexible tools that can easily be edited and manipulated. Some of the basic manipulations are:

▼ **Select.** To select a path, click on it with the **Path Adjuster** tool. When you select the **Path Adjuster** tool, all paths display with outlines. A selected path is displayed with control boxes around it.

91

FIGURE 7.4

*Feathering
a selection.*

▼ **Multiple selections.** To select more than one path at a time, hold down the **Shift** key while clicking on each one, or perform a marquee selection by clicking and dragging over several paths. Each selected path displays its control points.

▼ **Deselect.** Click anywhere on the image where there is *not* a selection. To deselect just one of several selected paths, hold down the **Shift** key while clicking on the one you want to deselect.

▼ **Delete.** To delete a path, select it with the **Path Adjuster** tool and press **Delete**.

▼ **Resize.** Select the path, then drag one of the control handles. Holding the **Shift** key while dragging a cor-

ner handle proportionally resizes an image.

▼ **Move.** Select a path, then drag it to a new location.

▼ **Skew.** Hold down the **Command** key while dragging a side handle.

▼ **Rotate.** Hold down the **Command** key while dragging a corner handle.

Figure 7.6 gives you an idea of what these manipulations look like.

Editing Freehand Paths

You've just spent a lot of time drawing a complicated path, but you're off by a hair in one area or another. Do you curse, throw things, and keep trying? Well, that's one option. Another option is simply to edit.

To edit, select the path with the **Path Adjuster** tool. Then choose the **Outline Path** tool, making sure the **Freehand** radio button is checked on the Controls palette. Hold down the **Shift** key and redraw the segment you want to change. When you release the stylus and

FIGURE 7.5

From top to bottom, strokes from the Grainizer, Big Masking Pen, Masking Airbrush, Masking Chalk, Masking Pen, and Single Pixel Masking brushes.

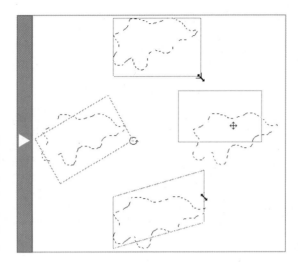

FIGURE 7.6
Clockwise from the top, resizing, moving, skewing, and rotating a path.

Select **Magic Wand...** from the Edit menu. You'll see the Magic Wand dialog box, and your cursor becomes a magic wand. This tool selects areas based on the hue, saturation, and value of the pixels. You can use it to select either solid colors or an entire range of colors.

93

Shift key, the path is redrawn with your correction.

A Little Bit of Magic

You have this great painting with lots of detail, but you want to use masks on all of the yellow areas to apply some finishing touches. Do you (a) spend all day trying to draw tiny little masks around these areas? (b) just forget about the finishing touches and walk away from the piece? or (c) select the **Magic Wand** tool from the Edit menu to handle this challenge with a few clicks?

If you answered (a) or (b) to this question, you should give the folks at Fractal Design Corporation more credit. If you answered (c), Merlin better move over, because you're now armed with your own magic wand.

Click your wand in the area you want to select, and the area is marked with the mask overlay color. To select a range of colors in an area, click and drag the wand. (You may have to work with this one to get the desired effect.) If you're selecting a solid area, click **OK**, and your area is masked.

If you're selecting a range of colors, use the **HSV** sliders to indicate the range you want. Click **OK** and your area is masked. Figure 7.7 shows the Magic Wand dialog box and a masked area.

THE PATH LIST PALETTE

 The image window selection icons are also available from the **Path List** icon on the

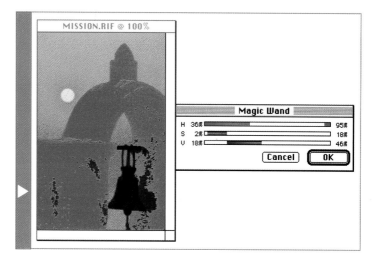

FIGURE 7.7

Using the Magic Wand to mask a range of colors.

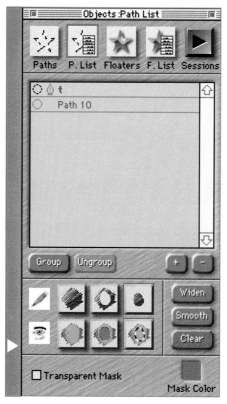

FIGURE 7.8

The extended Path List palette.

Objects palette, shown in Figure 7.8. The top of the palette displays a list where you'll see the names of paths in an image.

The symbol to the left of each path name indicates the type of path (selection, outline, or Bézier). Click on the icon to select the path. Double-click on the path name to open an informational Path Attributes dialog box that describes the type and location of the path. If you'd like to rename a path, this is the place to do it.

To group paths, select the ones you want (using the **Shift** key). The selected paths are highlighted. Click **Group**, and the grouped paths can now be worked with as a single item. To add a path at a later time, simply drag its name on the list into the group. To remove one, drag it out.

To convert a path to a selection, select **Convert to Selection** from the **Selection** cascading menu on the Tools menu. To change selected paths to curves, select **Convert to Curves**.

You are already familiar with the Drawing and Visibility icons on the bottom of the palette.

Click on the **Transparent** button to make your image visible through the selected mask color. To change the color of the mask itself, click on the color square (lower right of the palette), and select a new color from the color picker that is displayed.

If the corners of your path seem too sharp, click the **Smooth** button. The more you click this button, the smoother your corners will be, as in Figure 7.9.

You can actually cut a path in a path. (No, that's not a typo.) Several times, as a matter of fact. In other words, you can cut holes in existing paths to open an area or create layered effects.

Add an intersecting path to an existing one, then make it a negative path by clicking on the **Negative (–)** button. Negative paths work only when a positive path is present. Negative paths must be on top of the positive paths,

Create layered effects by making multiple cutouts and adding positive paths within negative ones (use the **Positive (+)** button). Negative paths have a red outline; positive paths have a black outline. Figure 7.10 shows cutout paths.

95

FIGURE 7.9

*Smoothing a path. The far left image is transformed into a smoother one as the **Smooth** button is clicked.*

FIGURE 7.10
*A path
with a cutout.*

THE PATH LIBRARY

Painter provides a library of preset paths and allows you to save libraries of your own creation.

Open the Path Library drawer, shown in Figure 7.11. To select a path, simply click on it and drag it onto your image. Open new libraries and save objects into libraries in the same way you would use any other Painter library. One of the library options, **Open EPS**, allows you to import EPS files from other programs, including Freehand and Illustrator as paths.

FLOATING SELECTIONS

Floating selection have many advantages:

▼ They let you work with multiple objects—items can be worked on, moved, and layered independently, making photo and image composition a breeze. Floating selections stay active, even when deselected, until you determine otherwise.

▼ Floating selections can be masked, painted into or around, manipulat-

FIGURE 7.11
*The Path
Library
drawer.*

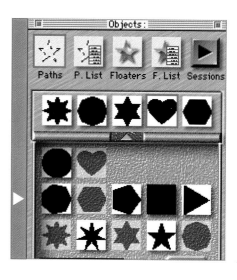

ed (scaled, rotated, distorted), and saved in libraries.

Floating selections are created from selections or mask layers. If you would like to keep your floaters in your image available to use at a later date, you must save your files in Painter's native RIFF file format. Otherwise, floating selections are automatically composited into the background.

USING FLOATING SELECTIONS

 Just as paths are selected and manipulated with the **Path Adjuster** tool, floating selections are selected and manipulated with the **Floating Selection** tool.

Creating Floating Selections

Floating Selections can be created from an image that can be selected with any selection or masking tool. Select the item, and make sure it is displayed using the **Visibility** button on the far right (with a marching ants marquee), not as a mask (blocked out with a solid color).

 Click inside the selection with the **Floating Selection** tool to

float it. It is placed on the Floater List palette, shown in Figure 7.12.

The item list contains all floating selections in a document. The currently selected item is listed in boldface. You may perform a number of actions from this list:

▼ **Select a floater.** Another way to select an item is to click on its name on the list.

▼ **Delete a floater.** You may delete a floater by selecting its name on the list and pressing **Delete**.

▼ **Rename a floater.** To rename a floater, double-click on its name. Enter a new name in the Floater Attributes dialog box, and click **OK**.

▼ **Group.** Use this button to group floaters. Hold down the **Shift** key and click on the names of each of the floating selections you want to group. Click on the **Group** button, and the grouped selections are now listed under a group label in the item list. You may change a group's name (the same way you change an item's name), and you may have multiple groups.

97

▼ **Ungroup.** Click this button to ungroup a selected group of floaters.

▼ **Show Selection Marquee.** Check this option to display a selection marquee around a selected floater.

▼ **Trim.** Select this button to remove any excess space from around a floater.

FIGURE 7.12

The extended Floater List palette.

98

▼ **Expand.** This button adds space around a floater, giving you room to feather it.

▼ **Collapse.** Use this function to turn a group of floaters into a single floating selection.

▼ **Restore.** Click on this button to reverse changes made with a masking brush.

Dropping Floaters

Floaters continue to float, even when deselected, until you specify otherwise. You can save your files with floaters, but if you'd like to have a floater merge with the background image, click **Drop** on the Floater List palette. **Drop All** drops all floating selections at once.

Manipulating Floating Selections

Floaters are very easy to work with and very easy to manipulate. Select them with the **Floating Selection** tool, and deselect them by clicking anywhere else in your image. Use the same click-and-drag technique to move a floating selection as you would any other selected item.

Delete a floating selection from your image by selecting it and pressing the **Delete** key.

To duplicate a floater, select it, hold down the **Option** key, and drag the duplicate to its new location.

Floating selections can also be layered, grouped, and composited using the Controls palette.

▼ **Layering.** The buttons on the left control the layering of floaters. Clicking on **Back** moves a floater to the back, or bottom, layer; **Front** moves it to the front, or top, layer. The **<<** and **>>** buttons incrementally move selections to the back (bottom) or front (top), respectively.

▼ **Opacity.** This slider makes a selected floater more or less transparent.

▼ **Feather.** This slider adjusts the feathering on the edges of a selected floater.

▼ **Composite Method.** You may select from a number of compositing options on this pop-up menu to determine how floaters interact. To composite images, select the floater you want to composite. If you are compositing it with another floating selection, make sure it is under the selected item. Otherwise, the selected floater is composited with the background layer.

▲ *Default.* The floating selection covers the image below it.

▲ *Gel.* This option tints the image below it using the color of the top image.

▲ *Colorize.* Colorizes the underlying image using the HSV values of the top image.

▲ *Reverse-Out.* Provides a drop-out effect, using negative color values (for example, black turns to white, yellow turns to blue, and green turns to purple) where the images intersect.

▲ *Shadow Map.* The bottom image is seen through a shadow of the top image.

▲ *Magic Combine.* Combines the top and bottom images based on luminance values.

▲ *Pseudocolor.* Turns the luminance of a floater into hue.

You can change your compositing method at any time, until a floating selection is dropped. Each time you change your compositing method, the new method replaces the old one. Figure 7.13 shows the compositing methods.

Item Masking

 This top row of icons determines how an item is displayed in relation to its mask.

 Masking Disabled turns off the masking data.

 Masked Inside masks the image inside the mask.

 Masked Outside masks the image outside the mask.

Figure 7.14 shows all three options.

Into Image

 This bottom row of icons determines how a floater is integrated into the background image.

 Unmasked leaves the selection unaffected by the background mask.

 Masked Inside lets the selection show outside the background mask.

 Masked Outside lets the selection show inside the background mask.

Figure 7.15 shows all three options.

FIGURE 7.13

Clockwise from the top left, the seven compositing methods: Default, Gel, Colorize, Reverse-Out, Shadow Map, Magic Combine, and Pseudocolor.

100

FIGURE 7.14

The Item Masking options from left to right: an item unmasked, masked inside, and masked outside.

Drop Shadows

You can automatically create a drop shadow for floating selections. Select the floater or group you want to shadow and choose **Drop Shadow...** from the **Objects** cascading menu (on the Effects menu).

In the Drop Shadow dialog box shown in Figure 7.16, enter the horizontal (x) and vertical (y) offset, radius (length of shadow), angle of light that casts the shadow, and thinness (fade-out) you want the shadow to have.

Click **OK** and your floater or group has a shadow, as in Figure 7.17.

The shadow is actually another floater that automatically groups with

the top floater. If you would like to have the shadow automatically merged into the original floater, click **Collapse result to one layer** in the Drop Shadow dialog box.

FLOATER LIBRARY

 The Floater palette, shown in Figure 7.18, is basically a library for your floating selections.

To place a floater in the current library, select the floater with the **Floater Selection** tool. Hold down the **Option** key and drag the image onto the palette. Enter a name in the Save Item dialog box, click **OK**, and your

FIGURE 7.15

The Into Image options from left to right: an item unmasked, masked inside, and masked outside.

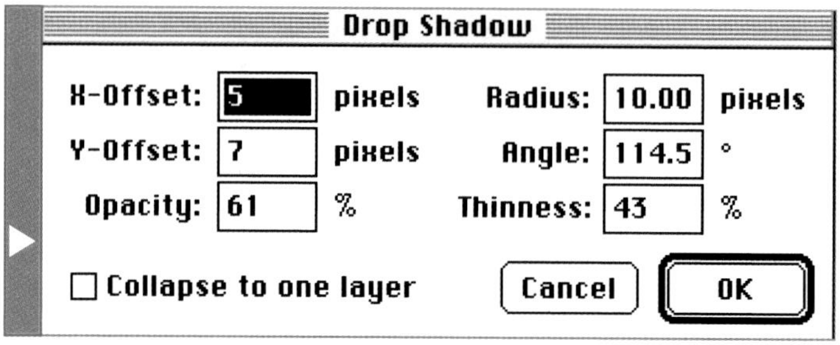

Drop Shadow

X-Offset: **5** pixels   Radius: 10.00 pixels

Y-Offset: 7 pixels   Angle: 114.5 °

Opacity: 61 %   Thinness: 43 %

☐ **Collapse to one layer**   Cancel   OK

FIGURE 7.16
The Drop Shadow dialog box.

selection is now included in the current library.

To delete an item from the palette, click on it and press **Delete**. Open and save new libraries as with any other Painter library.

GENERATE MASK

Painter automatically generates masks for floating selections. Select the item to be masked, then choose **Auto Mask...** from the **Mask** cascading menu on the Edit menu. Select a setting from the pop-up menu, click **OK**, and your floater is masked.

IMAGE HOSE

The **Image Hose** is a brush that paints with a series of

images, called a *Nozzle*. Each item in a series has its own mask that allows you to have the same control over the appearance of the hose images as you have over any floater. Painter comes with six preset Nozzles, and you can create your own from any Painter images.

Two palettes control the use of the Image Hose: the Brushes palette and the Nozzle icon on the Brush Controls palette, both shown in Figure 7.19.

FIGURE 7.17
A drop shadow.

FIGURE 7.18

The Floater palette.

and select one. Select the **Nozzle** brush on the Brushes palette (as you would any other brush), and begin painting with it, as in Figure 7.20.

There are several variants on the Brushes palette:

▼   **Size (Small, Medium and Large)** controls the spacing between elements in a Nozzle.

▼   **Random Spray** places images in a random (rather than linear) fashion.

103

USING THE IMAGE HOSE

To use a Nozzle, click on the **Library** button on the Brush Controls:Nozzle palette

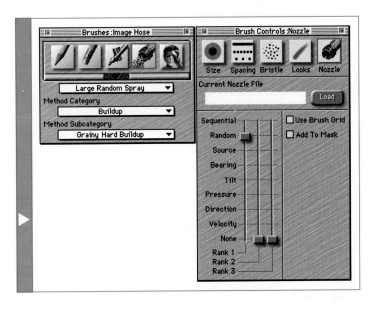

FIGURE 7.19

The Nozzle options on the Brushes (left) and Brush Controls palette (right).

▼ **Sequential Linear** deposits images in a linear fashion in a particular sequential order.

▼ **Random Linear** sprays elements in a linear fashion, but in random order.

▼ **Directional** places elements according to the directional specifications on the Size and Spacing palettes. These images are placed in a linear manner.

▼ **Small Luminance Cloner** uses the luminance of a cloned image for a nozzle.

Use the **Opacity** slider on the Controls palette to make a nozzle spray more transparent or opaque.

Decreasing the Grain slider adds the currently selected secondary color to the nozzle spray.

CONTROLLING A NOZZLE

You can fine-tune a nozzle using the settings on the Brush Controls palette.

▼ **Sequential** sprays images from the hose in the order in which you created the nozzle.

▼ **Random** sprays image in no particular order.

▼ **Source** sprays a nozzle file according to the luminance of a source file.

▼ **Tilt** applies a nozzle file based on the tilt of your stylus, providing your stylus supports tilt.

▼ **Pressure** sprays smaller elements with a lighter touch and larger images when you apply heavier pressure.

▼ **Direction** places items according to the direction of your brush stroke.

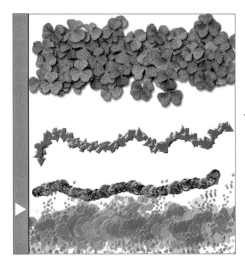

FIGURE 7.20

Using the Image Hose.

▼ **Velocity** deposits images according to the speed of your stroke.

▼ **None** only applies the last image in a nozzle file.

▼ **Use Brush Grid** applies a nozzle file based on a grid.

▼ **Add to Mask** places the nozzle spray onto the current mask layer.

CREATING YOUR OWN NOZZLES

You can create a nozzle out of any photographic or painted image in Painter. These images must first be made into floaters before they can be added to a nozzle file.

Open a new image window with these specifications: 500 pixels by 500 pixels and a 75-dot-per-inch resolution. Drag any floaters you want to place in the nozzle from the Floater library into this window.

Floaters must be individual, not grouped. To ensure this, click the **Collapse** button on the Floater List palette. Click **Trim** to make sure there is no excess space around any floating selection.

The order of appearance on the Floater List palette determines the sequence of the images in the nozzle file. Arrange the floaters in the order you want, then select them all and click **Group**. From the Tools menu, select **Make Nozzle from Group...** on the **Image Hose** cascading menu.

Painter creates a new image window with the nozzle elements in it. Select the **Save** option from the File menu, and save the image as a RIFF file in the Nozzle folder (inside your Painter 3 folder).

To use your new nozzle, simply load it from the Brush Controls palette.

Making a Nozzle from a Movie

You can take the frames from a movie and turn them into a nozzle file. Open the movie file, and select **Make Nozzle from Movie...** from the **Image Hose** cascading menu.

Painter creates a new image window with the movie frames in it. Select the **Save** option from the File menu, and save the image as a RIFF file in the Nozzle folder (inside your Painter 3 folder).

PRACTICE SESSION

1. Sketch out the beginnings of a self portrait, or any face, for that matter. Don't forget to give yourself the hairdo you always wanted to try but were afraid to.

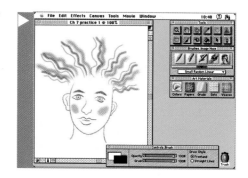

2. Select the **Outline Pen** tool, click the Freehand radio button on the Controls palette, and cut a mask around the face and hair. If you need to adjust the edges, hold down the **Shift** key while redrawing a segment.

3. Turn on the mask by selecting the center **Visibility** icon and the center **Drawing** icon on the image window icons.

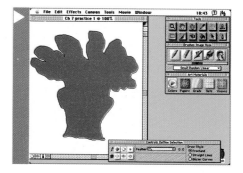

PRACTICE SESSION CONTINUED

4. Select the **Image Hose** brush on the Brushes palette. Change the variant to **Large Random Spray**. Use the **Image Hose** icon on the Brush Controls palette to open the Nozzle library. Select **Splat!** as your nozzle and click **OK**. Spray the images over your masked drawing.

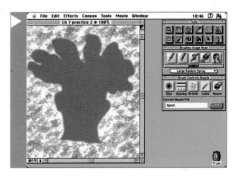

5. Switch back to the **Outline Pen** tool, and select the **Bézier** radio button on the Controls palette. Use this tool to create a curvy **selection** over the right side of your drawing. If you need to edit it, simply adjust the control points using the **Path Adjuster** tool.

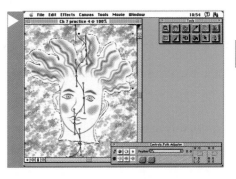

6. Open the Path List palette and make sure the curve you just drew is selected. From the Tools menu, open the Selection cascading menu and choose **Convert to Selection** to change your curves into a selection. Choose the **Negative** option from the **Tonal Control...** cascading menu on the Effects menu.

PRACTICE SESSION CONTINUED

7. Turn on the grid using the icon on the upper right of the image window. If you want to adjust the width and height of the grid, select **Grid Options...** from the Canvas menu and change the coordinates.

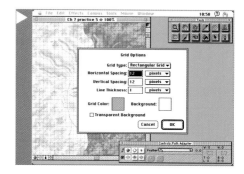

108

8. Open the Floaters palette and pull the leaf onto your image. If you need to size it, use the **Scale** option on the **Orientation...** cascading menu (on the Effects menu). Select one of the compositing methods. In this image, we used **Reverse-out**. Finally, copy the leaf around the edge of the image, using the grid to place it. The easiest way to do this is to hold down the **Option** key while dragging the floater to its new position (the original is left in its position).

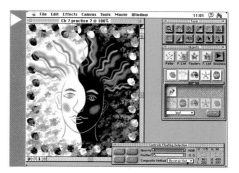

Clones and Scanned Images

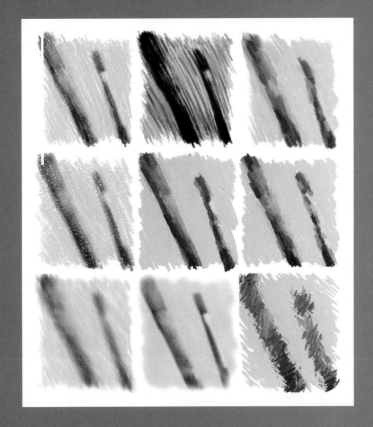

CHAPTER 8

CLONING AROUND

A *clone* is an exact copy of an image used to metamorphose images to any medium, apply special effects, combine elements, and trace photographs. Although it seems complicated, cloning is a simple process: Create a clone (exact copy) of an image, then use Painter's bells and whistles to transform the copied image into one using a different medium.

Painter accepts scanned and manipulated images from many popular photo retouching, color, and paint programs, including ColorStudio, Sketcher, and Photoshop.

CLONING AN IMAGE

Any time you want to use a cloning feature, whether a brush variant or a menu option, you must first create a clone of your image.

Open an existing image to be used as your source image. Select **Clone** from the File menu, and your image is duplicated. Figure 8.1 shows an image and its clone.

If you look carefully, you'll see the source image is named "Piece of Can." The clone is named "Clone of Piece of Can."

When you are working with cloned images, you must leave *both* the source and clone documents open, since the clone is "mapped" (linked) to the source.

110

FIGURE 8.1 ▶

Cloning an image. The source document is on the left, the clone on the right.

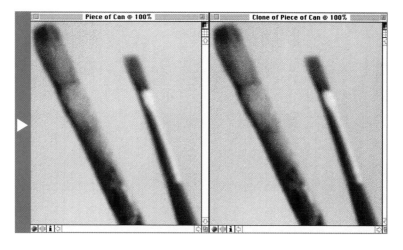

If you close your source and clone images, then later reopen them, you'll have to reestablish the link. To do this, open the source document using the **Open** command from the File menu. To select, clone, and link it to the source document, hold down the **Option** key while selecting **Clone** from the File menu. Choose the clone document from the open dialog box. The first image you opened is the source, and the second one is the clone.

If you already have your two images opened, choose **Clone Source** from the Options menu, select the name of the source from the pop-up menu, and your second image becomes the clone.

USING CLONER BRUSHES

When using a Cloner variant from the Brushes palette, you may either clone entire images or select parts of an image to be cloned.

To select a part of an image, open both your source and destination documents, making your source image active. (There are two best ways to make an image active: click on its title bar, or select the name of the document from the bottom of the Windows menu.) Select a **Cloner** variant from the Brushes palette. Hold the **Control** key while clicking on the source image. The place you click determines the center of the area cloned.

111

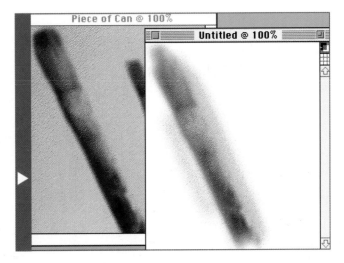

FIGURE 8.2

A source image (left) and a few strokes in a clone using the Soft Cloner brush variant (right).

Make your destination (clone) document active, then begin painting with your **Cloner** brush. Figure 8.2 shows a source image and a destination image with a few strokes of a Cloner brush.

You may select either a part of an image, or an entire image to re-create an image with any **Cloner** brush. When you use these brushes, you control the placement and direction of your brush strokes. Remember, you must keep your source image open while working with a **Cloner** brush. Let's briefly go over your Cloner brush variants.

CLONER BRUSH VARIANTS

Any variant that uses a Grainy method reacts well to the selected paper texture. You may also look at the method to determine what Cover method a variant uses. As with other brushes, you may use any or all of the customization techniques described in Chapter 4 to adjust Cloner brush variants to your specific needs.

Figure 8.3 shows the source image we are using in these examples.

Chalk Cloner. This variant lays down strokes like

the **Artist Chalk** brush and reacts very well to paper texture.

Driving Rain Cloner. This variant clones an image as though it were being viewed through the rain.

Felt Pen Cloner. This variant clones an image using felt pen strokes. Like the **Felt Pen** brushes, strokes from the **Felt Pen Cloner** build up and get darker as you apply them.

Hairy Cloner. This variant clones an image with strokes like the **Hairy Brush** variant, showing bristle lines and reacting to paper texture.

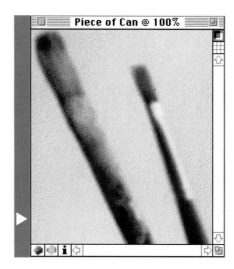

FIGURE 8.3

The original image.

Hard Oil Cloner. This variant clones an image using oil paint strokes with a hard edge. This is a cover brush using a Grainy method, so it covers underlying strokes and reacts to paper texture. Each time you lay down a stroke, a dotted line is displayed on your image. Wait until the line renders into a stroke before beginning your next stroke, or you won't get the results you want.

 Impressionist Cloner. This variant clones images with short, multicolored strokes like the **Impressionist** variant of the **Artist** brush.

 Melt Cloner. This variant clones an image using drippy, smeared strokes.

 Oil Brush Cloner. This variant clones an image using oil paint-like strokes with a soft edge. Each time you lay down a stroke, a dotted line is displayed on your image. Wait until the line renders into a stroke before beginning your next stroke, or you won't get the results you want.

 Pencil Sketch Cloner. This variant clones an image using pencil strokes.

 Straight Cloner. This variant clones your image without any changes—it *exactly* reproduces the source image.

 Soft Cloner. This variant clones an image with soft-edged, airbrush-like strokes.

 Van Gogh Cloner. This variant clones with multicolored strokes, like the **Van Gogh Artist** brush variant. You get better results if you use short strokes. Each time you lay down a stroke, a dotted line is displayed on your image. Wait until the line renders into a stroke before beginning your next stroke, or you won't get the results you want.

AUTO CLONE

If you have already tried some of the **Cloner** brushes, you may have discovered that it can take a long time to cover a large area. If you want Painter to handle some of the work for you, you can use the Auto Clone feature.

Set up your source and destination files and select the brush variant you want to use. You may clone an entire image, or select a portion of it. If you are not using a Cloner brush, variant, select **Use Clone Color** on the Colors palette so your brush uses the colors from your source image.

Select **Auto Clone** from the cascading **Esoterica** menu, found under the Effects menu. Your image is automatically cloned using the selected brush variant, as in Figures 8.4 and 8.5. Painter continues adding paint to your image until you stop the Auto Clone process by clicking anywhere in the image.

Auto Clone works best with the **Driving Rain**, **Seurat**, and **Van Gogh** variants.

TRACING PAPER

Painter's cloning feature also works like tracing paper—you can trace over an image, then get rid of it when you're finished. Use the image to be traced as the source, and create a clone automatically.

Make the clone (destination) document active, select all or part of the image you want to trace, and press **Backspace** or **Delete**. The selected area is deleted, but it is still mapped to the source image, as in Figure 8.6.

114

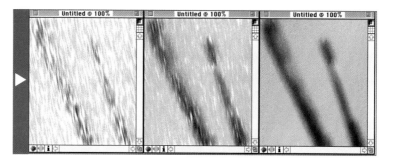

FIGURE 8.4
Using Auto Clone with the **Driving Rain** *variant.*

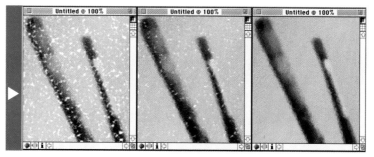

FIGURE 8.5
Using Auto Clone with the **Seurat** *variant.*

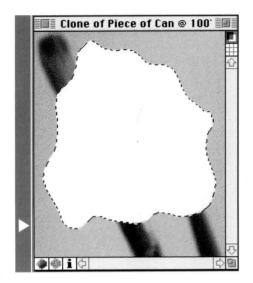

FIGURE 8.6

Selecting a tracing area.

Select **Tracing Paper** from the Options menu, and a nonprinting "ghost" of the image is displayed, as in Figure 8.7.

Paint over the tracing paper using any tool. When you are through tracing, turn off the **Tracing Paper** option. The ghost is removed, but your traced strokes remain, as in Figure 8.8.

115

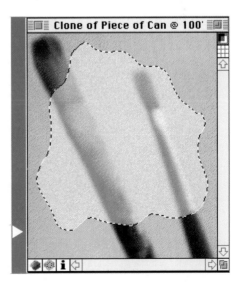

FIGURE 8.7

Turning on
Tracing Paper.

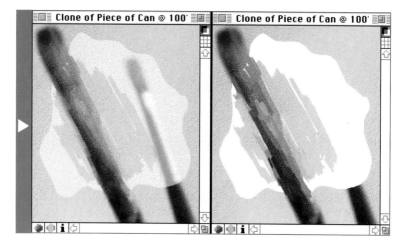

FIGURE 8.8

*Place your strokes (left), then turn off the **Tracing Paper** option (right).*

Recording Sessions and Resizing Images

CHAPTER 9

Painter can literally record your brush strokes and special effects to be saved for playback at a later time.

If you've ever created a drawing at 72 pixels per inch, then sized it up to, say, 300 pixels per inch, you may have been disappointed in the blurry, imprecise results. However, if you record the lower-resolution session, then play your brush strokes back at a higher resolution, your problem is solved! Painter re-creates your image at the higher resolution, complete with rescaling your brushes, paper textures, masks, and many effects.

Recording is very helpful if you're creating an image with repeated brush strokes. Simply record the stroke or strokes, then play back the session.

This feature is also very handy for teaching or demonstrating. Instead of recreating your examples, record them the first time, and play them back *ad infinitum*.

This feature works just like tape recording. Start the recording, stop it when you're done, then play it back when needed. It's really that simple. (Are we surprised?)

Recording session options are available on the bottom of the Tools menu as well as from the **Sessions** icon on the Objects palette, shown in Figure 9.1. The palette controls work just like the controls on a VCR: **Stop, Play, Record, Pause,** and **Advance** (from left to right).

RECORDING AND PLAYING BACK INDIVIDUAL BRUSH STROKES

This feature is great if you have multiple strokes to apply, and you want to take advantage of the electronic medium you are using. Just let Painter do it for you.

You must have a file opened to record a brush stroke.

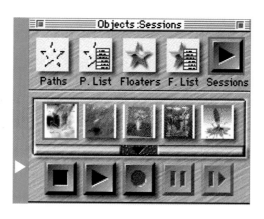

FIGURE 9.1 *The Sessions icon on the Objects palette.*

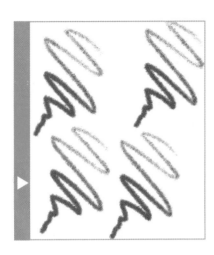

FIGURE 9.2

Playing back a recorded brush stroke.

deselecting **Playback** from the Tools menu (and uncheck it).

The color and brush variant of a recorded stroke changes according to the currently selected variant and the current color on the Colors palette. For example, if you record a stroke using the **Artist Pastel Chalk** variant in blue, then change your selected variant to the **Feather Tip Airbrush** variant using green, your recorded stroke changes accordingly. Figure 9.3 shows the recorded stroke played back using different brush variants and colors.

Select **Record Stroke** from the Tools menu.

Make any brush stroke you want, and the stroke is automatically recorded.

STROKE PLAYBACK

To play back the stroke, select **Play-back Stroke** from the **Brush Stroke** menu, then click where you want the stroke to appear in your image. The stroke replays each time you click, as in Figure 9.2.

When you are through playing back your stroke, stop the playback feature by

119

FIGURE 9.3

Playing back the stroke using different variants and colors.

PLAYBACK WITHIN MASKS AND SELECTIONS

You can confine your stroke playback to a mask selection. When you do this, strokes are automatically applied using a random pattern.

Select the area to which you want to apply random strokes. Then choose **Auto Playback** from the Tools menu. When the selection is filled to your satisfaction, as in Figure 9.4, click once, and the playback stops.

If you make your selection using the **Selection** tool, strokes may sometimes extend beyond the selected area, as in the left side of Figure 9.5. If you don't want this to happen, make your selection using the **Outline Pen** tool, as in the right side of Figure 9.5.

RECORDING AN ENTIRE SESSION

There are quite a few reasons to record an entire work session. Some are:

▼ For playback at a higher resolution.

▼ To reuse techniques in other projects.

▼ To have a record for teaching or demonstrating.

▼ To have a record of how you created an effect.

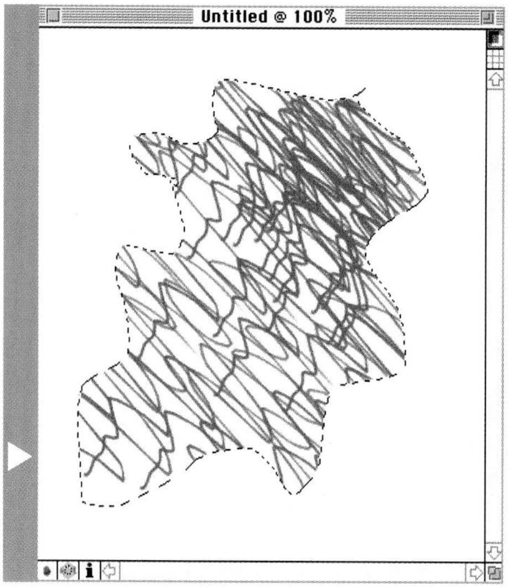

SESSION OPTIONS

Select **Session Options...** from the Tools menu. The Session Options dialog box, shown in Figure 9.6, is displayed.

If you check **Record Initial State**, the session is recorded intact, including the brush variants, colors, and paper textures used during the session. The currently

FIGURE 9.4

Filling a mask selection using Auto Playback.

120

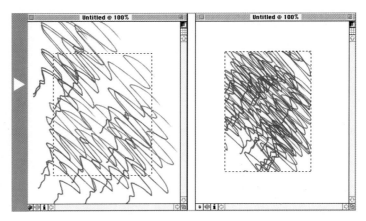

FIGURE 9.5

Strokes may extend beyond a selection made with the **Selection** *tool (left). To avoid this, use the* **Outline Pen** *tool (right).*

selected brush variant, color, and paper texture do not affect the playback.

If you uncheck **Record Initial State**, the playback is dependent on the currently selected brush variant, color, and paper texture.

If you would like your session to be recorded as a movie, select the **Save Frames on Playback** option, and specify how often (in *n*ths of a second) you'd like frames saved.

the special effects you want—Painter keeps track of them. When you are through with your session, click the **Stop** button.

Enter a session title in the Name the Session dialog box that is displayed, and click **OK**. Your session is now added to the current library. There is no limit to the number of sessions you can record.

RECORDING A SESSION

Click the red **Record** button on the Object:Sessions palette and begin making your brush strokes. Change variants, colors, and textures, and add all of

FIGURE 9.6

The Session Options dialog box.

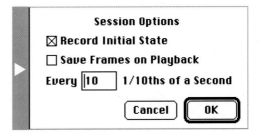

Session Options

☒ **Record Initial State**

☐ **Save Frames on Playback**

Every [10]   **1/10ths of a Second**

[Cancel] [**OK**]

SESSION PLAYBACK

When you are ready to play back your session, open the icon drawer on the Objects: Sessions palette, as in Figure 9.7. You'll see icons for the finished product from each session you have in the open library.

Select the session icon to play back, close the drawer, then click the **Play** button. Painter replays your session.

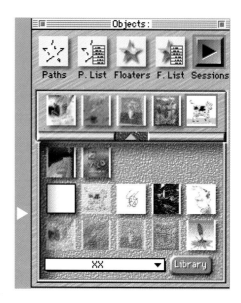

FIGURE 9.7

The library drawer on the Object:Sessions palette.

If you want to cancel a session while it is in progress, press **Command+.** (the period).

PLAYBACK AT A NEW RESOLUTION

You may record at one resolution, then play back at another, but you must follow a specific set of steps for it to work properly.

Recording

Open a new image file, and choose **Select All** from the Edit menu. Click the **Record** button, then choose **Deselect All** or draw inside the selected area. Begin your work and save your session as usual.

Playback

Open a new image file with a different resolution but same dimensions. Choose **Select All** from the Edit menu, then click on the **Play** button. Your session is replayed in the selected area.

RECORDING A SESSION AS A MOVIE

You can turn a recorded session into a movie and export it as a QuickTime movie.

Before you record your session, make sure **Save Frames on Playback** is checked in the Record Initial dialog box and specify how often you would

122

like frames saved. The more often you save frames, the smoother your movie will be. However, more frames result in more disk space used, so you'll want to take that into consideration.

Record a session as usual, select its icon from the Library drawer, and click the **Play** button to replay it. You'll see a dialog box asking you to name the frame stack for the movie. Enter a name and location and click on **Save**.

In the New Frame Stack dialog box, enter the storage type and the number of onion skin layers you want, and click **OK**. Your session is now saved as a frame stack. To save the stack as a QuickTime movie, use the **Save As...** function under the File menu to change the file name and file type.

CREATING LIBRARIES OF SESSIONS

As with many of Painter's features, you can create libraries of recorded sessions, organized in any way that suits your working habits.

NEW LIBRARIES

To start a new library, select **Playback Session...** from the Tools menu. The Recorded Sessions dialog box, shown in Figure 9.8, is displayed.

Click **Open Library...**, and the standard Apple File Open dialog box is displayed. Click on **New**, and enter a name for the new library in the Create File dialog box. Enter a file name and and click on **Save**.

OPENING A LIBRARY

To open an existing Library, click the **Library** button on the Sessions icons drawer, or click **Open Library...** on the Recorded Sessions dialog box.

123

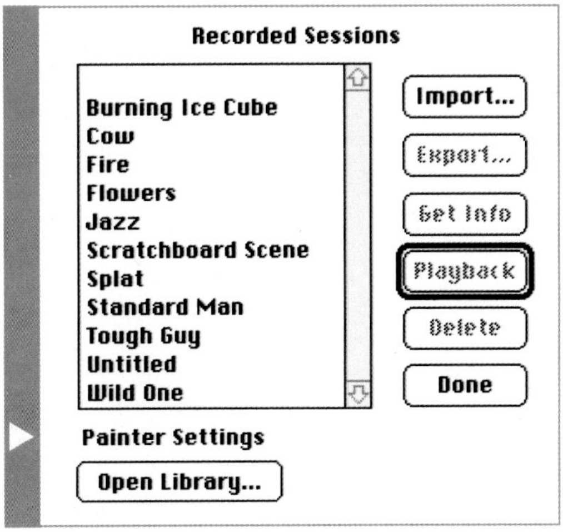

FIGURE 9.8

The Recorded Session dialog box.

Recorded Sessions

Burning Ice Cube
Cow
Fire
Flowers
Jazz
Scratchboard Scene
Splat
Standard Man
Tough Guy
Untitled
Wild One

Import...
Export...
Get Info
Playback
Delete
Done

Painter Settings

Open Library...

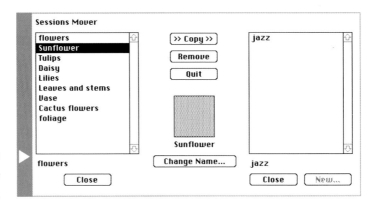

FIGURE 9.9

The Session Mover
dialog box.

From the File Open dialog box select the library you want to open. Click **OK**. You may now select and play back any session saved in that library.

EDITING LIBRARIES

You may append, move, and delete entire libraries or library contents using the **Session Mover**. Select **Session Mover...** from the **Movers** cascading menu under the Tools menu. The **Session Mover**, shown in Figure 9.9, is displayed.

Edit and append your libraries as required, and click on **Quit** when you are through.

124

PRACTICE SESSION

1. Select **Session Options** from the
    Brush Stroke menu, and make sure
    the **Record Initial State** option is
    checked. Since we are going to
    record a session at one resolution,
    then recreate it at a higher resolu-
    tion, open a new file (5 inches by
    5.5 inches) at 72 pixels per inch.

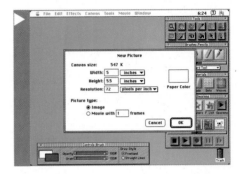

2. Choose **Select All** from the Edit
    menu, then click on the **Record**
    button on the Objects:Sessions
    palette.

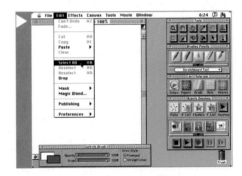

3. Begin painting a sunflower. Use a
    variety of colors, brushes, textures,
    and effects.

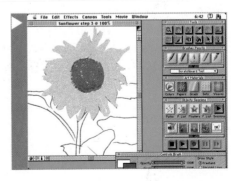

PRACTICE SESSION CONTINUED

4. When you are through with your painting, click on the **Stop** button. Create a new document with the same dimensions, but at a higher resolution of 300 pixels per inch.

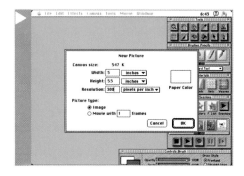

5. Choose **Select All** from the Edit menu, then immediately click on the **Play** button. Select the icon for the **Sunflower** session you just created, click the **Play** button, and watch it play back at a higher resolution.

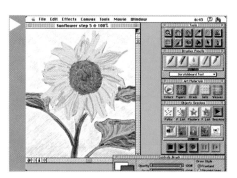

Movies and Animation

CHAPTER 10

You can use any of Painters tools and special effects to enhance any movie or animation or to create your own. Your work can be based on video, illustration, or both.

For the most part, everything you learned earlier in this book can be applied to movies. There are a few simple rules and exceptions, which are covered in this chapter.

Painter works with QuickTime and frame stacks to create animations, so let's go through the basics of those first.

QUICKTIME

QuickTime is a Mac extension file that lets your computer support sound, video, and animation. It also lets you export to Windows systems. Painter takes QuickTime data and turns it into a Painter frame stack. Painter frame stacks can be exported into QuickTime files for use with Mac or Windows video-editing software.

FRAME STACKS

A *frame stack* is a series of images in Painter that make up a movie or animation.

Images in a frame stack can be numbered. They must be numbered sequentially, with the number preceded by a period (**.**). Each numbered file must use the same number of digits. If you have less than 10 numbered files, you can use the format **Movie.1** through **Movie.9**. However, if you have more than 10 numbered files, 21, for example, you must use the format **Movie.01** through **Movie.21**.

OPENING MOVIE FILES

Use the same procedure to open a Painter movie or QuickTime file as you would any other Painter file. You are asked to give the file a new name, name the file, then click **OK**.

You'll see a dialog box asking how many layers of onion skin you'd like in your file. This refers to the onion-skin paper traditionally used by animators. This paper allows animators to see a number of frames at once through layers of transparent paper, so they may

FIGURE 10.1

Selecting the number of onion skin layers.

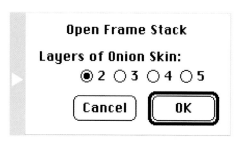

Open Frame Stack

Layers of Onion Skin:

◉ 2 ○ 3 ○ 4 ○ 5

Cancel   OK

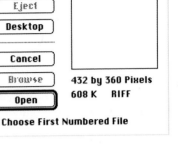

FIGURE 10.2

Opening numbered files.

align with and view previous frames as they create new ones. Painter allows the use of two to five layers of onion skin. Select the number of layers, as in Figure 10.1, and click **OK**.

Painter automatically saves changes made to a frame once you move to another frame. It is a good idea to always duplicate your file or save your file to another name before making any changes.

OPENING NUMBERED FILES

If you are opening numbered files, click the **Open Numbered Files** checkbox on the bottom of the Open dialog box, shown in Figure 10.2. You are prompted to select the first file in the sequence; do that and then click **Open**. Next, you'll be asked to select the last file in the sequence. Select it, click **Open**, and select the number of onion skin layers, as above.

129

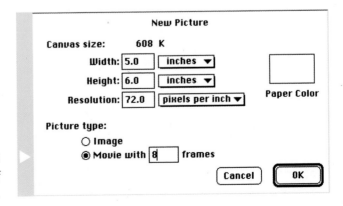

FIGURE 10.3

Selecting the number of frames in a movie.

CREATING A NEW MOVIE

To start a new movie file, select **New** from the File menu, and select dimensions, file size, and paper color, as with any other Painter file. From the **Picture Type** section, select **Movie with ____ frames**, and enter the number of frames you want your movie to have, as in Figure 10.3. Click **OK**, and name the file. Click **OK**, and in the dialog box shown in Figure 10.4, enter the number of onion skin layers and file storage type.

Images in a frame stack must be of equal size and resolution. They can be saved in the following ways:

▽ 256-level gray (8-bit gray)

▽ 256 Mac color palette (8-bit color)

▽ 32,768 colors plus a mask layer (15-bit color and a 1-bit mask)

▽ 16.7 million colors plus an anti-aliased mask layer (24-bit color and an 8-bit mask)

Simply begin adding images to your frames. In addition to the controls on the Frame Stacks palette (see below), you may use the **Page Up** and **Page Down** keys to move from frame to frame.

Use the first four options on the Movie menu to add frames, delete frames, erase contents of a frame (or range of frames), and go to a specific frame.

THE FRAME STACKS PALETTE

The Frame Stacks palette is displayed any time you open an existing movie file or create a new one. This palette, shown in Figure 10.5, displays a thumbnail of each movie frame, the number of frames in the current movie, the number of the current frame, and button controls that work much like the controls on your VCR.

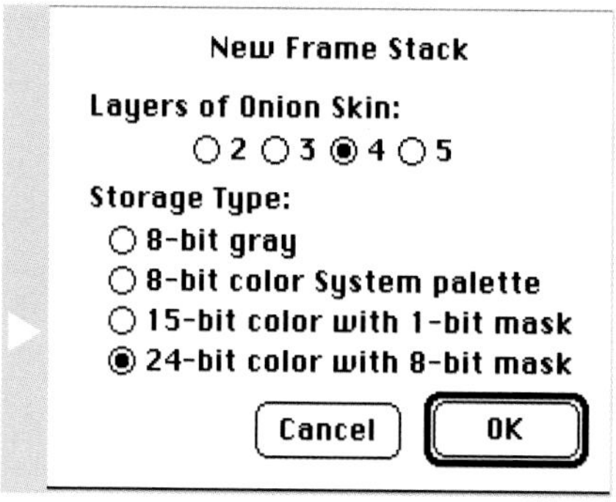

FIGURE 10.4 ▷

Selecting the number of onion skin layers and file storage type.

New Frame Stack

Layers of Onion Skin:
○ 2　○ 3　◉ 4　○ 5

Storage Type:
○ 8-bit gray
○ 8-bit color System palette
○ 15-bit color with 1-bit mask
◉ 24-bit color with 8-bit mask

[Cancel]　[**OK**]

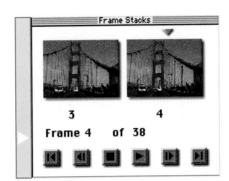

FIGURE 10.5

The Frame Stacks palette.

textures, masks, and special effects, either frame-by frame or to the entire movie.

To use a tool on a particular frame, simply go to that frame, and use it as you normally would.

131

To apply a special effect, texture, or brush stroke to an entire movie, begin recording a session, apply your effect and then stop recording the session. Make sure the movie is open, then select **Apply Session to Movie...** from the Movie menu. Select the session you want to apply, and click **Playback**. Your special effect, texture, or brush stroke is applied to the entire movie.

You can also use Painter's cloning tools with individual frames in a movie. Just remember that your frame dimension and resolution must be the same for the source and clone images.

You can use the cloning tools to create Tracing Paper, as well as any of the cloning brushes. You may also use the masking tools to protect portions of an image and replace the unprotected part with a cloned image.

Go to the first frame. You may also use the **Home** key.

Go forward, one frame at a time. You may also use the **Page Down** key.

Stop playing. You may also use **Command-.** (period).

Play the entire movie.

Go backward one frame at a time. You may also use the **Page Up** key.

Go to the last frame. You may also use the **End** key.

APPLYING YOUR TOOLS TO MOVIES

You can apply any of Painter's standard tools to a movie, including brushes,

Outputting Your Art

Eastern Light Sunflowers. Painting courtesy of Dennis Orlando.

CHAPTER 11

Well, this is it. You've learned almost everything there is to know about creating artwork in Painter. Now all you need to do is output your work.

Your selection of output is as important as your artwork. If you don't produce final copy that does justice to your work, your work isn't going to have the impact it should.

You have a variety of options for output, and the technology is now growing to a point where you can even output your art directly to watercolor paper or canvas! (See the last section of this chapter for some incredible options.)

134

Painter supports any PostScript or QuickDraw device. Many of the better options involve expensive equipment, but most metropolitan areas have service bureaus that provide access to these high-end machines at per-piece costs (you may also use nonlocal service bureaus via overnight shipping or high-speed modem).

We'll cover most of your options, but please check with your service bureau or the manual for your printing device for specific instructions on file type and page setup requirements.

COLOR MONITOR CALIBRATION

A key issue with any digital art is monitor calibration. Your artwork is created on a monitor that most likely will not provide a completely accurate color match with your output. Light reflecting off a printed medium and off a computer monitor are perceived differently by the human eye. There are a number of color-calibration devices available if color accuracy is an important issue for you. Most artists, however, are quite satisfied with proofing their work to a color printer, rather than calibrating their monitors every week.

EXPORTING FILES

Painter files are created and saved using the RGB color model. To place illustrations in many page-layout programs, you *must* use CMYK files. While Painter can't edit your files to CMYK, you may open Painter files in most color retouching or photo editing programs (such as ColorStudio, Digital Darkroom, or Photoshop) and edit them there.

Decide which file format works best with the program into which you'll

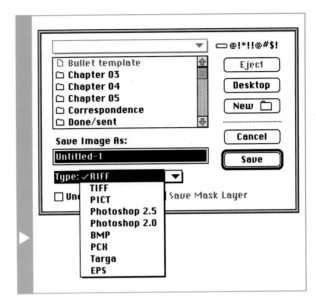

FIGURE 11.1

The Save As… dialog box with exporting options on the pop-up **Type** *menu.*

be importing Painter files, and select that format from the Save As… dialog box. Select **Save As…** from the File menu, and you'll see the dialog box in Figure 11.1. Select an exporting option from the Type pop-up menu, enter a file name in the **Save Image As** field, and click **OK**.

Your exporting options are:

▼ **RIFF** (raster image file format). This is the default option. Select the RIFF format to toggle the **Uncompressed** option. To save file space, always leave the **Uncompressed** option unchecked.

▼ **TIFF** (tagged image file format). A versatile graphics format that stores a map specifying the location and color associated with each pixel. TIFF is supported by IBM-compatible and NeXT systems.

▼ **PICT** Collections of QuickDraw routines needed to create an image. It is the main format used by the Macintosh clipboard.

▼ **Photoshop** (version 2.0 or 2.5). The native file format for Adobe Photoshop files. Photoshop files are always full 24-bit color.

▼ **BMP** Bitmap files are the main format used by the Microsoft Windows (IBM-compatible computers) clipboard.

▼ **PCX** (Picture exchange). A format used by many scanners and paint-style programs.

▼ **Targa** A file format used by high-end, PC-based paint programs. Targa files can have 8, 16, or 32 bits per pixel.

▼ **EPS** (encapsulated PostScript). Painter's EPS files conform to the EPS-DCS 5-file format, used for desktop color separation. Please note that files saved in this format *cannot be reopened* by Painter. If you want to be able to reopen a file saved in this format, save it in another format (with another name) *before* saving it as an EPS file.

136

Selecting **EPS** opens the EPS Save As Options dialog box, shown in Figure 11.2.

▲ *Hex* (ASCII) *Picture Data*. Select this option for programs, such as PageMaker, that require it.

▲ *Suppress Dot Gain*. This option enables Painter's dot gain adjustment.

▲ *Suppress Screen Angles*. This option enables Painter's screen angle adjustment.

▲ *Clip Path Frisket*. Select this option to save only the portion of an image inside a frisket. A frisket must be active for this option to be enabled.

▲ *Use Page Setup Settings*. This option disables Painter's default printer settings: 133 lines per inch, standard screen angles, and 16 percent dot gain.

▲ *Spot Type*. Select a dot,

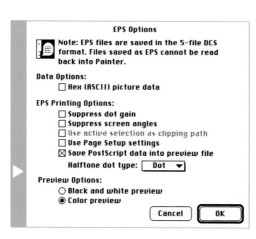

FIGURE 11.2

The EPS Save As Options dialog box.

line, ellipse, or custom shape for your halftone screen grid. The **Custom** option lets you create your own shape using a PostScript command. You must know the PostScript language to do this.

▲ *Save PostScript data into main file.* This option saves a printable preview of your EPS document. When this option is selected, the radio buttons for color or black-and-white previews are enabled.

PAGE SETUP OPTIONS

In addition to the file type, you may select from a number of page setup options for your images. To access

these options, select **Page Setup** from the File menu. You'll see the dialog box shown in Figure 11.3.

Paper Type, **Printer Effects**, and **Orientation** are relatively self-explanatory and are found as page setup options in most Macintosh programs. **Printer/Press Dot Gain** adjusts the size of halftone dots according to the requirements of your print shop.

Monitor Gamma refers to the brightness of your monitor. Unless you're using a monitor calibration device or you have a monitor that has other gamma requirements, you're pretty safe with the default setting. **Spot Type** determines the shape of your halftone dots.

Use the fields in the **Halftone Screens** area to change the settings for the grid of dots printed when using

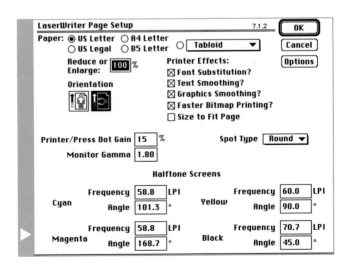

FIGURE 11.3 ▶

The Page Setup dialog box.

halftone screens (**Frequency**), or the angle at which the screens lay on your image (**Angle**). These settings may be adjusted for all four colors in the CMYK process.

IMAGE RESIZING AND RESOLUTION

Before outputting an image, you may want to change its dimensions (often called *resizing*) or resolution (often called *resampling*) to fit your output device. When outputting your work, the relationship between the image size and its resolution is very important.

Resolution refers to the numbers of *pixels per inch* (ppi) displayed on your monitor, or the number of *dots per inch* (dpi) used in the printing process. Most monitors have a resolution of about 72 ppi; typical laser printers have a resolution of 300 dpi and can go as high as 600 dpi; imagesetters can have resolutions of 1,200 dpi to more than 5,000 dpi; and most color printers range from 260 dpi up past 300 dpi.

We'll say it again: *Read the device user manual or contact your service bureau to determine the exact resolution requirements.*

Select **Resize...** from the File menu to access the Resize dialog box shown in Figure 11.4.

The lower half of the box provides you with current information about your document, including its dimensions and resolution. The current size refers to the amount of RAM your image takes up, not to the amount of hard disk space it uses.

To resize your image, enter new values in the **Width** and **Height** fields. Change the resolution of an image using the **Resolution** field. Use the pop-up menus next to these fields to change the units of measurement for your image. Click on the **Constrain File**

FIGURE 11.4

The Resize dialog box.

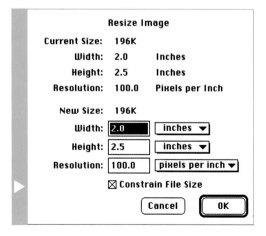

Size box to keep your document from taking up any additional memory.

When you have resized your image, click **OK** to accept your changes.

You can also find out your image size and resolution by clicking on the **i** in the lower left of your document window (next to the frisket icons). The pop-up box, shown in Figure 11.5, also shows how your image fits on the page size selected in the Page Setup dialog box.

When increasing the resolution of an image by large leaps and bounds, you may occasionally get fuzzier results than you would like. To avoid this, use the record and playback method for increasing image resolution, discussed in Chapter 9.

Writer printing conventions and are relatively self-explanatory.

The four bottom options allow you to select from the four printing methods supported by Painter.

▼ **Color QuickDraw.** Use this option for printers that use QuickDraw (color or black-and-white), such as many ink-jet printers. Dot gain and halftone screen options do not apply to QuickDraw printers.

▼ **Color PostScript.** Check this option if you use a PostScript printer (most color laser printers, thermal wax printers, imagesetters, and dye-sublimation printers). Dot gain and halftone screen settings apply.

139

PRINTING

Once you have determined the size, resolution, and page setup options for your image, select **Print** from the File menu to open the Print dialog box, shown in Figure 11.6.

Most of this dialog box follows standard Apple Laser-

FIGURE 11.5

*Clicking on the **i** in the lower left of your document window displays image size, resolution, and placement.*

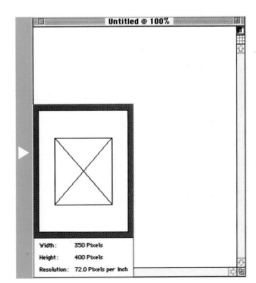

Untitled @ 100%

Width:	350 Pixels
Height:	400 Pixels
Resolution:	72.0 Pixels per Inch

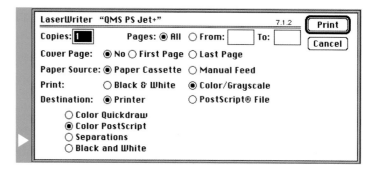

FIGURE 11.6

The Print dialog box.

▼ **Separations.** Use this option if you want to print color separations (usually done on an imagesetter) directly from Painter. If you are using your own device, please check your documentation for specific page setup settings. If you are using a service bureau, please contact it for specific instructions before outputting files. This will save them a lot of aggravation due to incorrect settings, and will eliminate unnecessary delays.

▼ **Black and White.** This option applies to users of black-and-white laser printers.

When you have made your selections, click **OK** to begin printing.

OUTPUT OPTIONS

There is a large assortment of printer types available on the market today, some of which are affordable, and others that are generally more cost-effective if used through a service bureau. You'll have to carefully weigh your needs with cost considerations: black-and-white PostScript laser printers and ink-jet color printers start at less than $1,000, and go up to several thousand dollars; color laser copier systems begin around $60,000; used imagesetters begin at around $10,000, new ones at $70,000; thermal wax printers range from a couple of thousand dollars to more than $10,000; dye-sublimation printers begin where thermal wax printers leave off; and Vutek systems (used to print directly onto gessoed canvas) begin at $500,000 (no, that's not a typo).

We'll briefly cover some of the options available, but due to technology that changes faster than the phases of the moon, we will not be able to cover it all.

We recommend reading the following section, contacting some printer companies for more information (*always* ask for print samples), and, most important, talking to other people in your field to get first-hand feedback on the advantages and disadvantages of a particular device that interests you.

LASER PRINTERS

Laser printers operate in a similar fashion to photocopy machines: A laser passes over a negatively charged drum, which then attracts negatively charged toner and is rolled over positively charged paper. The paper then passes through a heated roller to adhere the toner to the paper. (H*int*: This means if you get toner on your clothing or carpeting, you can wash it off with *cold* water. If you use hot water, the toner adheres to the textile as fiercely as if it were a piece of paper.)

Laser printers are available for black-and-white as well as color printing. Laser printers are not continuous-tone printers. To print grays or colors, they use a screen, and depending on the resolution of the screen, you'll likely notice the dots.

COLOR LASER COPIERS AS PRINTERS

A number of companies are now using color copiers, via a special raster image processor (RIP), to provide color output. The most prominent copier in this field is the Canon CLC using a Fiery RIP. This technology provides continuous-tone images (like a photograph, not using visible dots) and allows a little latitude in your selection of paper. However, thicker paper and highly textured paper may produce questionable results. Depending on the copier, your paper size will range from standard letter-size to legal- or tabloid-size paper.

A color laser copier produces very vivid, sometimes fluorescent, colors. If you are using one as a proofing device for an image that will be reproduced using process printing, keep in mind that process printing does not produce the same vivid results. The closest you can get to accurately reproducing some of these colors will be to print additional PMS colors over the process prints.

If you are simply using the color copier to produce limited edition prints, and are not interested in accurate color proofs, this is an excellent choice, although somewhat cost-prohibitive. Color laser prints are available from some service bureaus, but are not as common as other types of color prints that provide better color proofing for process color printing. We recommend Iris prints for final pieces and Match prints for color proofing.

141

THERMAL WAX TRANSFER PRINTERS

Thermal wax transfer printers work more like dot matrix printers than like laser printers. But instead of pins pressing against a ribbon, they press melted wax onto a page, and they are much quieter.

Most thermal wax printers provide 300-dpi, noncontinuous prints, with good color coverage. Although not entirely color accurate, they are generally pretty good proofing devices, especially considering that they are affordable enough for many of us to own. This is a good option for artists who do not have large corporate coffers to dig into, do not have large trust funds to tap, or have not (yet) won the lottery.

DYE-SUBLIMATION PRINTERS

Dye-sublimation printers work in a similar fashion to the thermal wax transfer method, except they provide continuous-tone color coverage. Rather than heat wax and transfer it directly onto the paper, dye-sublimation heats ink, which then turns into gas. The gas is sprayed onto the paper, where it returns to its solid form. Cool. It looks great too.

Results from a dye-sublimation printer provide photographic-quality

results (sometimes even better than photographs), particularly on smooth, glossy paper. A number of printers work well with a variety of media, including watercolor paper.

Probably the most famous of this type is the Iris printer. Most major service bureaus provide Iris prints. Most dye-sublimation prints, particularly Iris prints, are excellent proofing tools. Many dye-sublimation prints smudge and eventually fade when exposed to sunlight.

The catch: Beginning at $10,000 with a per-page print cost of as much as $5, dye-sublimation technology is prohibitively expensive for most artists and small companies to own.

INK JET PRINTERS

Ink jet printers use little nozzles to squirt ink onto your paper. The more expensive the ink-jet printer, the more sophisticated a method it uses to squirt the ink.

You get continuous-tone images, but usually with a lower resolution than dye-sublimation printers (as low as 180 dpi), and you have to wait for the ink to dry. Some models may experience clogging of their nozzles and may require special paper. They are generally *very* quiet machines.

There is good news: Color ink-jet printers can be had for less than $500—or can run up to $5,000. The lower-end ink-jet printers are slower, provide less accurate color proofing, and have a lower resolution, but you don't have to mortgage the farm to own one.

IMAGESETTERS

Imagesetters provide high-resolution (1,200- to 3,600-dpi) resin-coated (RC) paper or film to make plates for commercial process printing. They are frequently known by their brand names, including Linotronic, Varityper, or Agfa. At a price of $50,000-70,000 new, most of us will never own one, nor will we want to.

PRINTING DIRECTLY TO CANVAS

We've saved the best for last. There is one source we know of that prints your image directly onto gessoed canvas, using continuous-tone acrylic paint, at almost any size you could possibly need.

The 16-foot printer was originally designed for the outdoor (billboard) industry to provide continuous-tone 14-by 48-foot prints directly onto vinyl. The technology is manufactured and patented by Vutek (Meredith, New Hampshire—information on their agent is listed at the end of this section, they do not handle orders directly).

The company also makes a smaller 8-foot machine that is currently being used to transfer Painter images to canvas. The width of the canvas they stock is 5 feet, so they suggest paintings be kept at a maximum width of 4 feet, to allow extra canvas for stretching on frames. Since the canvas is on a roll, length is almost no issue. In fact, Richard Noble, who handles orders for the process, suggests paintings be no smaller than 6 feet in length, since that's the size at which the process really begins to shine. (He suggests Iris prints for smaller images.)

The ink is acrylic-based and sprays through four CMYK jets simultaneously. Since it was designed for the outdoor industry, the ink is extremely stable when exposed to sunlight and is excellent for archival pieces. You also have the option of applying a glossy overcoat or even manually reworking a painting, and the output is sturdy enough to be stretched. Figure 11.7 shows Richard Noble with one of his paintings that has been transferred to canvas and then stretched on a frame.

Substrates in stock include pre-gessoed, acid-free, cotton canvas, and some paper stocks.

143

According to Richard, images processed via this technology are 18 dpi. Yes, we said 18 dpi, not 180 dpi, not 1,800 dpi. (For the outdoor industry, the standard is 6 dpi—they have just pushed the envelope here to provide higher quality for fine art output.) We don't exactly understand that one, but we hear the results are incredible.

The low-dpi requirement allows file sizes to remain relatively small: a 3-foot-square Iris print at 150 dpi can easily run larger than 80 MB. At 300 dpi, the same file can easily run larger than 300 MB. A 5-foot painting at 18 dpi can run smaller than 5 MB; people have actually sent files that fit on floppy diskettes.

The process supports any file type that can be read by Photoshop and can handle images from either Macintosh or PC platforms. Images can be sent either on SyQuest cartridges or floppy diskettes, 18 dpi, with the dimensions you want for the final output.

Since this sounds too good to be real, we'll hit you with the best part: Prints are affordable. There's a setup charge of $35, a $30 shipping and handling fee, and a charge of $12 per square foot. This includes stock canvas or paper; special-order substrates are more. Actual print time runs an hour or two, but order turnaround takes two to four weeks. At $500,000, owning the technology is really out of reach, but at least the prints are affordable.

To order or receive more information, contact Richard Noble, Noble & Company, 899 Forest Lane, Alamo, CA 94507, phone 510-838-5524, fax 510-838-5561. Richard is the only authorized agent for the process worldwide.

FIGURE 11.7

Richard Noble and one of his paintings that has been printed on canvas, then stretched on a frame. Painting and photograph © Richard Noble.

144

Section II

Dennis Orlando

THE WILLOW POND

CHAPTER 12

ARTIST PROFILE

Traditionally trained at the Hussian School of Art in Philadelphia, PA, and Bucks County College in Newtown, PA, Dennis is an award-winning commercial graphic designer, creative director, and fine artist. He has spent more than 20 years working with water colors, markers, pastels, oils, and pen and ink. He is currently the creative director for K.I. Lipton Marketing Communications in Doylestown, PA.

In 1989, Dennis was instrumental in setting up one of the first Macintosh-based advertising agencies in the Philadelphia area, and he helped convince artists, printers, color separators, and clients that a new era was dawning.

Dennis' digital studies of Cézanne, Monet, and Picasso have convinced many that capabilities now exist for an artist to create masterpieces electronically. His digital paintings are stored on disk and magnetic cartridges and will soon be available on CDs.

Digital paintings produced by Dennis have been exhibited at computer shows in Los Angeles, San Francisco, Boston, and Philadelphia, and he plans to participate in upcoming gallery shows with both traditional and digital

artists. He is currently experimenting with multimedia applications for his art, and recently exhibited his work at the Michener Museum in Doylestown, PA.

To create his digital paintings, Dennis uses a Macintosh IIci with 20 MB or RAM, a 20-inch SuperMac color monitor with a 24-bit video card, Fractal Design Painter and X2 software, a Wacom ArtZ drawing tablet with a wireless stylus, and an EFI Fiery RIP connected to a Canon CLC 300 color laster printer.

ON USING PAINTER

My intention is to use the computer to create art. Not computer art. Just art.

I create my computer paintings in the same way I have created traditional paintings for the last 20 years. Only the tools are now electronic. The artist's tool should never get in the way of what the artist is trying to express. I've realized the artist creates with his heart and mind, not paint brushes. The computer is just a tool.

Experimentation is fun and healthy and should be considered a necessity. Filters and special effects can open up avenues of self-expression, when used appropriately. My belief is that all artists who learn to use these new tools will eventually discover themselves.

Style and technique will eventually evolve as individual artists find their own way down the digital highway.

THE WILLOW POND

The Willow Pond is actually the first in a series of paintings Dennis is creating from a photographic study he took in Doylestown, PA in the Summer of 1994. The painting featured in the step-by-step section on the following page is the oil paint version. Dennis has also completed a water color of the same scene, and he plans to continue with a series of pond subjects.

Dennis has developed a technique for his computer oil paintings whereby he gets the feel and look of applying a brush over the tension of a stretched canvas (see Step 2). He feels this is important because it allows him to see signs of his traditional work in his work on the computer.

149

FIGURE 12.1

The watercolor version of The Willow Pond.

STEP-BY-STEP

1. Dennis began *The Willow Pond* by drawing out the composition using the **Chalk** brushes to create an underlayer of color. He then worked in different areas of the painting to refine and develop his idea.

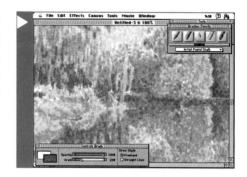

2. After placing the underlayer, he used the **Liquid** brushes to paint into and manipulate the chalk layer. He uses a technique that pushes and pulls the paint to create the painterly look that distinguishes his work. This is particularly noticeable in the water and sky of *The Willow Pond*.

3. Once the painting has reached a certain stage of completeness, Dennis applies Painter's **Sharpen** filter to intensify the brush strokes. Since the filter creates more of a contrast than he wants in his work, he uses the **Liquid** brushes to rework certain areas, particularly the sky and the reflection of the trees in the water.

150

PORTFOLIO

All of Dennis' digital paintings are done traditionally, by eye-to-hand using a technique hae calls Direct Digital Painting. He usually starts with a rough pencil/chalk sketch to set up the composition directly on the screen, and then lets the painting evolve from there. No art or photography has been scanned or manipulated to create any of his images.

STILL LIFE, WINE BOTTLES AND FRUIT, *a digital painting re-created from an earlier, traditionally created oil painting.*

MONET STUDY, FIELDS #1, *a digital fine art study inspired by the paintings of Claude Monet.*

PORTFOLIO CONTINUED

FLOWERS IN LIGHT AND SHADOW, a 1994 original digital painting. This 300-dpi painting started as a pastel drawing in Dabbler and kept evolving once imported into Painter. Dennis worked at it for more than a month, refining the detail and reworking the composition.

152

TYLER PARK, 1994, detail of a digital oil painting inspired by the beautiful fall foliage in Bucks County, PA.

PORTFOLIO CONTINUED

ISLAND DRIFTWOOD, a 1994 original digital painting. Dennis discovered this piece of natural sculpture while walking along a stretch of beach in Barbados. He found it inspiring and quite beautiful; it is one of those subjects he finds himself going back to draw or paint again and again.

153

Denise Devenuti

CIRCUS

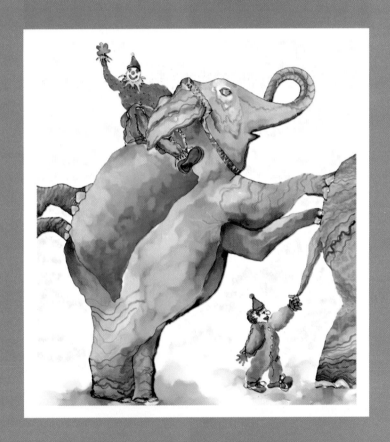

CHAPTER 13

ARTIST PROFILE

Although her parents didn't know it, they prepared Denise for a career as a computer artist almost from day one. Her mother, an artist, put a paintbrush in her hand at a very young age. Her father, one of the first computer specialists, exposed her to the new technology before most of the world even knew there was such a thing. In the late 70s, her family bought the first Apple computer that came on the market, but art software wasn't available at that time.

Denise studied art and advertising at Iona College in New Rochelle, New York. She began her career as a graphic designer at an ad agency, then took an eight-year detour into advertising, sales, and promotion. About a year and a half ago, she discovered the new art abilities of the computer, quit her job, and bought a Mac. Teaching herself and taking some classes at the School of Visual Arts and Parsons School of Design in New York City, Denise once again tapped into her creativity and merged it with the technology she learned about earlier in life.

Denise now does illustration, production, and designs screens for multimedia packages. Her clients include American Express and *Reader's Digest*.

Denise creates her art using a Mac Quadra 660AV with 24 MB of RAM, a 230-MB internal hard drive, an APS 1-Gig external hard drive, an APS optical drive, a CD-ROM drive, an 88-MB SyQuest drive, a Sony Trinitron 14-inch monitor, and an Apple LaserWriter 320. She proofs work using Iris prints from a service bureau.

ON USING PAINTER

My first feeling was that it was like having an art store at your fingertips. There are so many different things to try, and its like your imagination is your only limitation.

I really love water color and have worked with it traditionally. I can appreciate that you can take more risks with water colors on the computer, because when you put color down on traditional water color paper, you are really committing yourself.

Another thing I found very interesting was that you run into the same issues with Painter's Watercolor features as you would when you are doing it traditionally. For example, you have the same lack of control in blending colors with water on the computer as you would traditionally. It's very true to the natural medium. But on the computer you can change it if you don't like it.

Italy was the first piece I did on the computer. It was interesting to experiment with the different wet and dry layers. Even though I do most of the painting in one wet layer, when you dry a layer it takes on different properties because it allows the underlying layer to come through the next layer you apply. It just gives it a different look—it adds a whole new dimension to working with water colors.

I couldn't believe I was actually producing this on the computer. I had done both Italy and Circus traditionally and then redid them on the computer. I think both pieces came out better on the computer because I was able to take more risks and I was able to change them. With the use of the **Wet Eraser**, you can erase color you put down. If color bleeds outside an area, again you can remove it. The **Pure Water** brush lets you get really soft blends. Painter allows you a lot more control over water colors than you would normally have.

The only concern I had was trying to figure out what the color was going to look like when it's printed. The screen looks one way, then it looks another way when you change it from RGB to CMYK, then it changes again when you take it from an Iris print to offset printing. Now I refer to a Pantone book, which is helpful when you have large areas of color you want to control. The Pantone Process Color Imaging Guide 1,000 has a solid Pantone color, then next to it, it has what that color will look like when it's printed using the four-color process. There are so many Pantone books out there that it's easy to buy the wrong one, but this one makes it easy to get the color I want.

157

STEP-BY-STEP

1. Denise began her painting by scanning a line drawing into Photoshop and saving it as a PICT file. She opened it in Painter to use as a template, then converted it from 150 dpi to 300 dpi.

2. Before starting to paint, she chose the **Wet Paint** option under the Canvas menu. All of her work was done with a mouse using the **Watercolor** brush variants, primarily **Water Brush Stroke**, **Simple Water**, and **Pure Water** (to add water and blend color).

3. Denise mottled the elephants by first laying down a colored background and blending it with a size 50 **Pure Water Brush**. She used the **Wet Eraser** to remove any unwanted strokes. Since the **Dropper** tool is unavailable when the Wet Layer is active, she had to guess when she wanted to pick up a color.

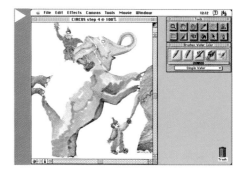

STEP-BY-STEP CONTINUED

4. After applying most of the color, she used the **Pure Water** brush to blend her colors. She used the **Wet Eraser** to clean up any ragged edges.

5. While still on the Wet Layer, Denise added finishing touches to the foreground of the painting. She used the **Wet Eraser** to remove any sketch outlines that showed through. She then dried the Wet Layer so she could apply a mask to the foreground elements.

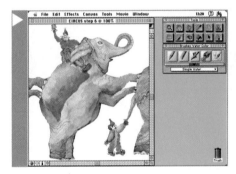

159

6. After applying the mask, Denise stroked the **Splatter** brush (at a size of 45) horizontally across her canvas, darkening the paint a bit at the bottom. She then dried the Wet Layer and resized the image.

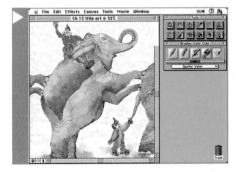

PORTFOLIO

ITALY, *a reworking of a traditionally painted water color created using Painter's* **Watercolor** *brushes with a mouse.*

SHELL, *created using Painter's* **Watercolor** *brushes with a mouse.*

Gary Clark

THE CROW'S ROAD

CHAPTER 14

ARTIST PROFILE

Gary is a professional artist and has been a professor at Bloomsburg University in Bloomsburg, Pennsylvania for 23 years, teaching computer graphics, drawing, and design. He has a BFA in graphic design, an MA in sculpture, and a Pennsylvania teaching certification. Gary is self-taught on the computer and has been creating computer art for about eight years.

Gary is represented by Silicon Gallery of Philidelphia *and* Agnisiuh Gallery of Sedona, Arizona. His recent exhibitions include a solo exhibition at the Russell Rotunda in the United States Senate Office Building (Washington, D.C.), a two-person exhibition at Silicon Gallery of Philidelphia. Pennsylvania, "Counterpoint" The 26th Annual National Juried Drawing, Photography and Printmaking Exhibition in Ingram, Texas and the "7th National Juried Art Exhibition" held at the Mable Cultural Center in Mableton, Georgia where his work won an award. He recently exhibited his work at the Michener Museum in Doylestown, Pennsylvania.

Gary creates his artwork using a Quadra 950 with 24 MB RAM, a 400 MB built-in hard drive and a 1-gigabyte external hard drive, a Wacom 12-x 18-inch graphics tablet, a 21-inch Apple color monitor with a RasterOps 224XLTV video board and a DayStar graphics accelerator, SyQuest 44 MB cartridge drive, a QMS 100-30i ColorScript thermal wax printer (in-house), and an LFR Laser Graphic slide maker (in-house). Gary uses a service bureau for Iris prints or photographic prints via 4- x 5-inch transparencies.

THE FUTURE

Gary is working on a project with Dr. Helmut Doll of the Department of Mathematics and Computer Science of Bloomsburg University. The official title of the project is "Fractal Landscape Generation, as Mathematics and as Art"; it was funded by the Pennsylvania State System of Higher Education Faculty Professional Development Council.

Dr. Doll is writing computer programs that will image fractal landforms and allow them to then enhance the resulting images with such attributes as light and shadow, texture, transparency, and point of view. When they have created visually significant forms, the forms will be rendered. Gary will then use the rendered three-dimensional landscapes as source material in new artwork and used with other programs such as Painter, Photoshop, and Alias Sketch. If the project is successful, the art will be framed and exhibited on the Bloomsburg University's campus and possibly elsewhere.

ON USING PAINTER

I first discovered Painter in a magazine review and then found a colleague at another university who had it on his machine, so I had a chance to play with it. It was just wonderful. It was an analogy to the natural materials I was used to and the interface was pretty straightforward, so it was natural to use. I use natural media now only to enhance what I do with the computer. Sometimes I'll make some studies with inks or dyes or paints, and I may scan those in and use them as part of the work. Or sometimes I'll use them underneath as a template and pull pieces up with the Cloning function.

I show my work, I sell my work. I've been showing nationally and internationally in a mix of traditional and computer art shows. I'm finding that traditional art shows have a lot of trouble finding where to include electronic art. My art might make it into a show as a drawing, as a photograph, or even as a print. I find it depends on the show prospectus how I'll enter the work. I'll even find myself calling to find out what their preferences are in terms of which category the work might fit into. One of my pieces was given a Purchase Award at the Larsen National Drawing Biannual at Austin Peay State University in Clarksville, Tennessee. It was the only computer drawing at the show.

I'm finding you'll have to read the perspective very carefully and have some alternatives for output—I may have the work printed as a photograph and again as an Iris print. Then, depending on the show, I pick the one that seems more suitable. At one show in Oregon, I won a prize and there were lots of favorable comments on the work, but the biggest comment was "Can you tell me what an Iris print is?"

I feel the public has the misconception that the computer makes the work and that you make thousands of prints, but nobody questions someone who makes a silk screen or an etching. So there's this idea that electronic art is infinite and that the computer creates it. I hope one of the things that I've helped to do is to change people's vision of what computer art is. The more people who see electronic art, the more it breaks their misconceptions that computer art is blocky and that the computer creates the art.

THE CROW'S ROAD

Gary produced this piece using a variety of techniques, including third-party filters, scanned color swatches, still video captures, and fractal-generated mountains, all combined to create an enchanting other-worldly look.

STEP-BY-STEP

1. Gary began by generating mountains in VistaPro, a fractal program. He saved the file as a PICT and brought the image into Painter. In Painter, he smoothed the mountains with the **Just Add Water** brush and applied color with the Chalk brushes.

164

2. To create the sky, he used an image from a still video capture, and he worked it with the **Just Add Water** and Chalk brushes, as in Step 1.

3. To add color and texture, Gary scanned in a swatch from a random-color tempera painting on water color paper. He keeps a library of these 8 x 10 swatches for when he needs to add color and texture. He applied a small piece of this high-resolution scan as the ground over a mask that fit the mountains. Using the **Just Add Water** brush, he blended the mountains into the ground and saved the file as a PICT.

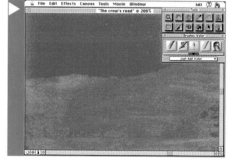

STEP-BY-STEP CONTINUED

4. In Photoshop, he applied almost-transparent tree and branch textures from another video capture. He isolated some of these images as a channel and added the same scanned tempera swatch as in Step 3.

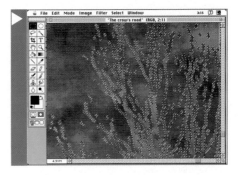

5. Again, saving the file as a PICT, he brought the image back into Painter and applied the **Lighting** filter to add the shaft of light. To finish, he worked into the painting, especially in the foreground, applied the thin border, and adjusted the contrast.

165

PORTFOLIO

Most of Gary's art is created by using a combination of Painter, Photoshop, and special effects filters. The landscape forms are generated using fractal mathematics and are pieced and colored in Painter using a variety of tools (Gary's favorites being the **Pastels**, **Distorto**, and **Watercolor** tools). He used the **Cloner** feature to modify the basic look of some of his pieces, and Kai's Power Tools for textures and gradients. His skies are shot with an RC570 Canon still video camera and then are composited in Painter. Each piece is different, and his method of working and selecting the final output is based on reactions to the ongoing process, his original idea, and how the final output is to be viewed. Gary believes that experience and experimenting are important, and he never finishes a work session without making many new discoveries.

IMMERSION, *a composite image created using many of the same techniques explained earlier in this chapter. Gary added a lot of hand drawing to the background of this piece.*

PORTFOLIO CONTINUED

POSTCARDS FROM THE DIGITAL HIGHWAY, STOP 1.

The first in a series created to make tangible the concept of the digital highway. Gary designed this ongoing series to take the viewer through tourist attractions on the digital highway.

POSTCARDS FROM THE DIGITAL HIGHWAY, STOP 2.

For most of the series, Gary used pieces from his swatch library to bring color and texture to the series. For this piece, however, he used the gray luminance levels from a swatch.

PORTFOLIO CONTINUED

POSTCARDS FROM THE DIGITAL HIGHWAY, STOP 3.

The head of the telescope was taken from a still video capture and softened with the **Pure Water** brush. Gary used a rectangular gradient fill from Kai's Power Tools to create the pole.

POSTCARDS FROM THE DIGITAL HIGHWAY, STOP 4.

The mountain forms in this series were created using KPT Bryce, a third-party product. Details were filled in by hand using the **Pastel** brushes.

Dorothy Simpson Krause

THE GOLDEN APPLE

CHAPTER 15

ARTIST PROFILE

Dorothy is a professor of computer graphics at the Massachusetts College of Art in Boston and Corporate Curator for IRIS Graphics, Inc. She has a Bachelor of Arts degree in Painting (Montevallo University), a Master of Arts degree in Art Education (University of Alabama), a Doctor of Education degree in Art Education (Pennsylvania State University), and a Certificate in Management of Lifelong Education (Harvard University).

Dorothy's recent exhibits have included solo shows at the New England School of Photography, IRIS Graphics, Inc., and the Center for Creative Imaging. Her work has been included in the Seventh National Computer Invitational, Digital Masters at the Ansel Adams Center for Photography, Pixel Pushers Exhibition of Digital Art, Siggraph 94, and Fractal Design Expo 94. Her work is on the January 1995 cover of IEEE *Computer Graphics and Applications* magazine and the February 1995 cover of *Computer Artist* magazine.

Dorothy's work is based on the premise that our similarities are greater than our differences and, at this time in history, electronic media enable us to transcend our separateness and to understand, as in no time in the past, our interdependence. She uses historical and contemporary images, maps showing voyages of exploration, the shifting boundaries of acquisition, and patterns of migration. She embeds in her images the fragments of written language, signs, symbols, charts, and diagrams that are also embedded in our consciousness. She enlarges their fragmented political, ethical, and social meanings by combining, layering, manipulating, and merging them into provocative statements or questions.

Dorothy creates her art using a Quadra 700, with 32 MB of RAM, a 1-Gigabyte hard drive, a WACOM tablet, a UMAX UC630 color scanner, a CD-ROM drive, and a SyQuest 44/88/200 cartridge drive. She works concurrently on two monitors, a 14-inch NEC MultiSync and a SuperMac 21-inch, keeping her images on the SuperMac and her menus and notes on the NEC. She proofs either to her HP550C color printer or Sharp JX730 color printer, and produces final output at IRIS corporate headquarters or at a fine arts IRIS printer like Cone Editions.

ON USING PAINTER

It's just fabulous because I like working back into my pieces using pastels and other tools.

170

I'll print something out, work with real media to try out some effects, then replicate those effects in Painter.

The **Just Add Water** brush is fabulous. It allows you to really do some wonderful transitions, smoothing of areas, to actually flow one thing into another. It's also wonderful to be able to apply textures selectively or to be able to clone using the original luminance of an image.

My work is becoming much more painterly and less photographic in quality, even though I'm still using photographic source images. I think it's actually going to change very dramatically in the next year because I was originally a painter and I really love that quality of Painter.

171

THE GOLDEN APPLE

Dorothy uses a lot of metallics in her pieces by using Kai's Power Tools, which she says allows for some incredible metallic effects when outputting to Iris prints. She may also go manually into a print to add additional metallic effects using metallic paint and gold leaf.

STEP-BY-STEP

1. Dorothy began her piece by opening two scanned images, Woman with Apple and Child with Book, an image she had previously made into a "pastel" with Painter. She selected the entire Woman with Apple image and copied it. She then selected the child's hair and pasted the Woman with Apple into the selected area, used **Edit Fade** to undo it to 50%.

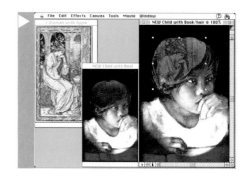

172

2. Dorothy filled Woman with apple with a gentle gold sweep from the metallic presets in Kai's Power Tools Gradient Designer. She used Painter's **Apply Surface Texture** feature, selecting **Image Luminance** and setting **Shiny** to **Off** to get an embossed effect.

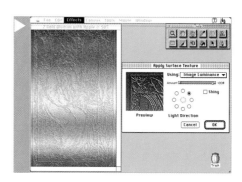

3. Opening Gold Woman with Apple in Photoshop, Dorothy ran the **Gaussian Blur** filter once at **1 pixel**, and the **Unsharp Mask** filter three times at **50%**, with a **Radius** of **1 pixel** and a **Threshold** of **0** to give it a heavier embossed quality. She selected the entire image and copied it. Opening

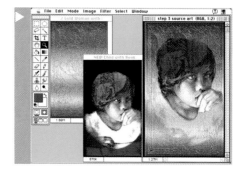

STEP-BY-STEP CONTINUED

Child with Book, Dorothy selected the child's face, hair, and hands (to protect them), and chose **Paste Behind** to put the Gold Woman with Apple around and behind the child.

4. Back in Painter, Dorothy selected the apple. Using Kai's Power Tools she filled it with **Gentle Gold Sweep** set on **Radial**. She saved the image as The Golden Apple.

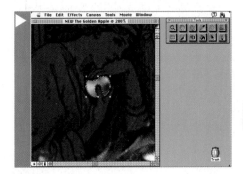

5. To finish the piece, she used the **Just Add Water** brush to smooth irregularities, then she used the **Artist Pastel** brush to add dark strokes to the hair and shadows.

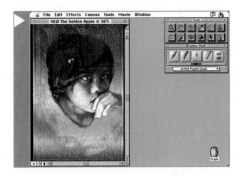

PORTFOLIO

By focusing on timeless personal and universal issues—hopes, fears, wishes, lies, dreams, immortality, and transience, Dorothy challenges herself and the viewer to look beyond the surface to see what depths are hidden. She wants her work to have the quality of allegory—not to be factual but to be truthful in charac-ter. She doesn't plan for any pre-scriptive messages; instead she invites individual interpretation of her work. In fact, she tries to combine almost incongruent images and loves it when viewers come up with interpretations she never thought of.

MESSAGES

PORTFOLIO CONTINUED

SHRINE OF FLOWERS ▶

THE BOOK OF HOURS ▶

David Locke Higgins

ALASKAN BROWN BEAR

CHAPTER 16

ARTIST PROFILE

David Locke Higgins is an internationally collected portrait artist. He is a graduate of the University of Michigan School of Architecture and Design with a degree in advertising and graphic design. He has been a professional artist and graphic designer for 40 years.

Historically, his portraits and illustrations have been created in gouache, oil pastels, and oil paints. David finds that the Mac, and in particular Painter, as a painting medium offers him greater expression of form, design, and color than any of the traditional materials with which he has worked.

The remarkable likenesses shown in this chapter are portraits of specific animals who reside in the San Diego Zoo and Wild Animal Park. David feels the closeness of the images allows the viewer to experience the character and personality of the animal with more intimacy than a full-body rendering in an environmental setting.

While the animals David paints are not all endangered today, each creature is potentially subject to the thoughtless encroachment of humans. Believing that each of us has a contribution to make to end the destruction, David dedicates his work to the preservation of all living things. A portion of all profits from his animal prints is donated to the Center for the Reproduction of Endangered Species.

David creates his art using a Mac VX with a Daystar 40/40 accelerator card, 36 MB of RAM, a 250-MB hard drive, a separate 75-MB hard drive as a scratch disk, and a Wacom 6- x 9-inch pressure-sensitive tablet. Original images are captured from life using a JVC videocam and ScreenPlay software. The reference image is placed on a second Apple 12-inch color monitor and the work is drawn on an adjacent 16-inch Apple color monitor. He proofs his work to an HP 550C color ink-jet printer, and he uses an Iris or Fiery printer for final output.

ON USING PAINTER

It is as immaculate as a program can be for fine art.

I wrote a letter to Fractal Design and said we must stop using the term "computer-generated art" because it's like saying the box of water colors creates the water color painting.

Painter is an art medium. It allows more freedom of expression in color and in not being uptight. In fact, I have trouble not leaving my paintings alone because I'm not afraid.

178

There's a freshness of technique that's possible that I never experienced in using the real material. So Painter allows me to do what I've always wanted to do.

The only thing it lacks is the smell.

ALASKAN BROWN BEAR

David spends many hours at the San Diego Zoo. He likes to think that the animals actually recognize and relate to him. Some of them do show recognition and will deliberately come over to him for attention. It is easy to read human characteristics and emotions into their actions.

In this painting, the bear had just come out of the water, so he was wet and shiny. He was approaching and begging for a treat. His eyes were sparkling and focused, and his lower lip was twitching in anticipation.

This particular piece was completed in one sitting.

STEP-BY-STEP

1. For this image, David chose **Cotton** paper from the Papers palette and a neutral gray-brown for the paper color. Using the **Big Rough Out Brush**, he began applying a thin wash with a reddish brown. He lets the paint dribble and make a mess within the confines of where the bear is going to be. He overlays that with an outline of the bear using the **Fine Chalk**, pretending he has a handful of pastels.

2. Next, he more broadly defines the lights, darks, and general color of the bear, using the **Chalk** brushes. He posterized the image at 12 levels, which is a neat way to introduce colors he would never dare think of using. He has a tendency to overwork, so he is careful to preserve the looseness of his lines. He smoothes the image with water.

3. To complete the image, he defines three oil brushes with 20 bristles each in small, medium, and large sizes to paint the wet fur. He posterized the image, again looking for surprise colors, inverted the image to find some complementary colors to weave into the shadows, at times having as many as three versions of the image open at once.

PORTFOLIO

BUBBLES *is a Sumatran Orangutan who was raised with people before coming to the Zoo. Sadly, she has a difficult time relating to the rest of the troop. Her expressions sometimes seem to reflect her isolation.*

181

SNOW LEOPARD *was familiar with David's presence at the zoo and in this portrait is approaching him.*

PORTFOLIO CONTINUED

SULAWESI HORNBILL.

This beautiful bird is very proud. He and his mate are wonderful to watch. It seems that they are aware of the visitors and will intentionally hold a pose to be fully appreciated.

182

SUMATRAN TIGER.

This beautiful cat lives in a carefully crafted enclosure with lots of logs and running water. She will interact with the visitors through the glass of the viewing area. It is a special experience to look right into her eyes.

Kerry Gavin

PUFFIN

CHAPTER 17

ARTIST PROFILE

Kerry graduated from Pratt Institute in 1972 with a BFA in printmaking and a minor in education. He served 4 years in the AirForce, ironically as a graphic designer. He worked in New York as a graphic designer for several publications and ad agencies before moving out on his own 15 years ago.

He is a publications designer and editorial illustrator, with clients that include *The Hartford Courant*, *The New York Times*, *The Boston Globe*, *The Chicago Tribune*, *Industry Week*, *Publishers Weekly*, *Byte magazine*, *Glamour*, *Ladies Home Journal*, *MacUser*, and many others.

Kerry uses a Macintosh Centris 650, a RasterOps 20T Multiscan monitor with a Paint Board Turbo video card, a 12" x 12" CalComp graphics tablet, a LaserWriter Select 360 printer for black-and-white proofs, and Iris color prints from a service bureau to create his digital paintings.

ON USING PAINTER

I've been using the computer in design for the last two-and-a-half years, mostly using QuarkXPress. For whatever reason, I just didn't want to make the jump to computer illustration. Up to then, I used primarily water color and pen and ink. In the last four years I shifted from traditional water color to adding airbrushing. Very recently—the last eight months—I began illustrating on the computer. The very first program I really tried working with was Painter. I read about it in a couple of publications, and it sounded like it was maybe a little more intuitive than some of the more techie-oriented programs, so I sent away for a sample disk.

I played around with it a little bit and really liked it because it was more intuitive. I really responded to that. I worked with it for a few months, and in that time I developed a dozen or so images.

I find that Adobe Illustrator is object-oriented—it uses shapes and forms—while Painter is very drawing oriented. So I sit down and draw and paint, which is something I haven't done in 20 years. It's a really different process. I feel that Adobe Illustrator draws on my design background, while Painter draws on my painting and drawing background.

PUFFIN

Kerry produced this piece as one of many for an ongoing series of installations of a novel appearing in *The Hartford Courant*. Kerry produces an illustration for each of three weekly installments. He works closely with author Colin McEnroe, rendering the illustrations as the chapter is being written. This fast pace sometimes requires him to use a modem, rather than overnight courier, to ensure the illustrations arrive at the newspaper by press time.

STEP-BY-STEP

1. Kerry began with a 200-dpi pencil sketch of the puffin. At this stage, he turned the puffin into a floating object so he could mask it and work around it.

2. Using the **Chalk** tools, he added color and detail to the bed, quilt, and night table.

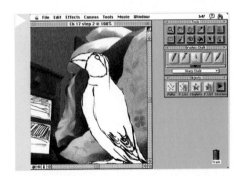

185

3. To finish the vignette, Kerry painted details into the puffin, wall, and shelving. He used the **Brightness** and **Tone** controls to enhance the image. For the deckled edge, he used a mask feathered to 10 that he has in his library for this series.

PORTFOLIO

It has been 20 years since Kerry sat down and painted, and he is surprised that he waited until he had a computer to do it. But since he has started to use Painter, he wants to sit down and paint strictly for enjoyment. Kerry says Painter is very intuitive, yet he doesn't know how many of its features could be re-created traditionally (for example, the ability to work with pastels by laying down masks).

The images that follow are also from the serial in *The Hartford Courant*.

HERONS

WRATH

PORTFOLIO CONTINUED

PEARS

HALLOWEEN

PORTFOLIO CONTINUED

ENGAGEMENT BAND.
Each of the musicians in this vignette was created from one image and given a separate instrument to get a uniform look.

188

THE MORNING. *For this vignette, Kerry actually painted American Gothic as a separate image, in full detail. He then placed, sized it, and skewed it to fit this image. He says it was worth the work because it was fun and worked really well.*

Susan LeVan

THE QUIET CONVERSATION

CHAPTER 18

ARTIST PROFILE

Susan has an MFA in printmaking and began her career doing editorial illustrations using traditional methods. Her husband and business partner, Ernest Barbee, is an architect and exhibit designer who has been working with Macs since 1984. In 1992 they began looking for a way to work together, and the computer seemed to be a logical connection, so they formed LeVan/Barbee Studio.

Susan uses a Macintosh Quadra 700 with 20 MB RAM, a 20-inch SuperMac display with a SuperMac Thunder Light graphics card, a 10" x 13" SD510c Wacom graphics tablet, and a Techtronics Phaser II SDX (in-house) or Iris prints (service bureau) to output her artwork.

ON USING PAINTER

In the Fall of 1992, we went to pick up some new computer equipment. The salesman was talking about tablets and how much he didn't like them. The minute he described it, I said "I have to try this thing." I sat down at a computer, and the program that was open happened to be Painter. I did a few quick cartoons, and I turned to Ernie and said, "I have to have this." We bought the program and tablet on the spot.

Two things were going on: All of my work, both fine art and illustrative art, is in mixed media. It became obvious that with this particular program, and other digital methods, you can mix all kinds of media that you can't mix in the real world. You can put down a swath of water color and cut through it with a scratchboard tool, erase it with an eraser, then paint over it with oil paint. It also seemed to be the answer to our finding a way to work together. Before the tablet and Painter, manipulating the mouse just didn't work for me.

There are so many possibilities with this program, technically, that it is good to start out doing what you know. Do not get caught up in the technical tricks. Explore it like any painting tool. Then, as you feel comfortable, start adding the extra textures and little gizmos you want. It is like any other tool, and needs to be driven by the artists' concepts of work they want to do, rather than by the technology.

THE QUIET CONVERSATION

The Quiet Conversation was created as a portfolio piece. Susan wanted to show people interacting in an everyday setting, using stylized figures. The text in the image is a sort of visual pun, as well as a sort of textural wallpaper.

STEP-BY-STEP

1. Susan began this image using the **Fine Tip Felt Pen** and **Simple Water** brushes. She used the **Rectangular Selection** tool to create the black boxes that became the bodies of the two figures. The baseline was drawn with the **2B Pencil** using a straight lines brush stroke. She began working the image with the **Large Chalk** and **Scratchboard Tool** brushes.

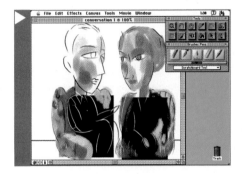

2. She continued to fill out the figures using the **Large Chalk** and **Sharp Chalk** brushes. She used the **Scratchboard Tool** brush to add detail to the bodies and chairs.

3. Susan began the background in dark colors with the **Large Chalk** brush, using the **Basic** and **Wriggles** paper textures. She followed this with warm grays on the Rougher paper texture, leaving the dark colors to bleed through the edges.

STEP-BY-STEP CONTINUED

4. To reinforce the feel and presence of a quiet conversation, Susan added text without letting it dominate the image. She cloned the file, chose **Select All**, **Delete**, and then **Tracing Paper**. She then wrote between the grayed images using the **Fine Point Pen** in black. The file was copied using the function on the Edit menu.

5. Susan pasted the text file into the original image as a floating selection. With the **Dropper** tool, she chose the background white of the floater, then she chose **Generate Mask: Current Color** from the Edit menu. From the Floating Selections palette, she chose the **Mask Inside** icon, changed the Opacity to **50%**, and dropped the now gray text into the image.

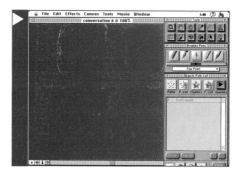

6. Again using the **Dropper** tool and **Generate Mask:Current Color**, she selected a gray from the text and dropped yellow into the image using the **Bucket** tool (with **Mask** selected on the Controls palette). She repeated this process several times with subtle variations of the gray tones until she was satisfied with the result.

PORTFOLIO

Susan now does all of her work with Painter. One of the things she likes about Painter is that it is completely intuitive and you don't have to be a computer genius to use it: You just have to start working with it—pick up the tool and use it—which is very appealing to artists. She says, "Painter has amazing depth. There is always some new discovery to be made. It's a lot like magic."

TWO HEADS *is one example of Susan's experimentation with unconventional (and what she calls "conventionally unpleasing") combinations of color to push an image in new directions.*

RED SQUIRREL *was created from observing the antics of Eastern Gray squirrels outside her window. She achieved the painterly collage feeling by layering the central image of the squirrel and overlapping multiple paper textures behind and below the subject.*

PORTFOLIO CONTINUED

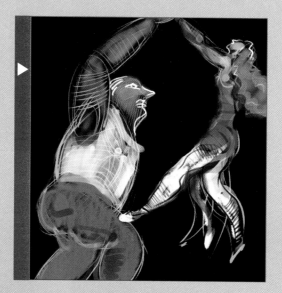

ACROBATS *was created on a black background using the* **Scratchboard Tool, Fat Airbrush, Fine Tip Felt Pen**, *and* **Simple Water** *brushes. In creating the white areas, she was looking for a translucent effect, as if using gouache. She got this effect by creating a negative of the file and painting in black with a* **Simple Water** *brush before again reversing the file.*

A BOY AND HIS GREY DOG, *exhibited at Fractal Design's ArtExpo 94 (at the Siggraph, MacWorld, and Seybold shows), was created using the* **Fat Airbrush**, **Default Crayon**, **Medium Felt Tip Pen**, **Scratchboard Tool**, **Large Chalk**, *and* **Simple Water** *bushes.*

Extensions and Third-Party Software

APPENDIX A

This appendix includes short reviews and descriptions of extensions and third-party software that may be used in conjunction with Painter. Retail prices suggested by the manufacturers are included, but if you shop around you'll probably be able to save some money.

SPECIAL EFFECTS

ADDDEPTH

This is an instant perspective application that allows users to create 3-D graphics in line art and type. It offers full support for Type I fonts, Adobe Illustrator, TrueType fonts, and Aldus FreeHand.

System requirements: Any color-capable Macintosh, 4 MB of RAM, and System 6.0.5 or later. *Suggested retail price*: $175.

Ray Dream, Inc., 1804 N. Shoreline Blvd., Mountain View, CA 94043. Phone: 415-960-0765, fax: 415-960-1198.

ADOBE DIMENSIONS

Extrudes, revolves, bevels, and manipulates 2-D images into 3-D objects and effects. It also integrates 3-D images into artwork from graphics programs.

System requirements: Macintosh SE or larger, including portables. *Suggested retail price*: $129.95.

Adobe Systems, Inc., 1585 Charleston Rd., Mountain View, CA 94039. Phone: 415-961-4000 or 800-833-6687.

ADOBE STREAMLINE

Converts high-resolution black-and-white or color bitmapped images into PostScript language art work. After an image has been converted, it can be edited, changed, or modified in a drawing or page-layout program.

Systems requirements: Macintosh Plus or larger, Adobe Illustrator. *Suggested retail price*: $195.

Adobe Systems, Inc., 1585 Charleston Rd., Box 7900, Mountain View, CA 94039. Phone: 415-961-4400 or 800-833-6687.

ALDUS GALLERY EFFECTS

Classic Art Volume I gives graphic effects to bitmapped images and scanned color or gray-scale scans. **Volume 2** emphasizes bold painting and drawing styles. **Volume 3** automatically transforms scanned photos into artwork. Uses classic painting and drawing methods.

System requirements: Macintosh SE/30, LC, or II family, 2 MB of RAM, hard disk drive, (Texture Art requires CD-ROM drive), color monitor and card, System 6.0.5 or later, 32-bit QuickDraw. *Suggested retail price*: Classic Art, Volume 1, $199; Volumes 2 and 3, $99.

EFFECTS SPECIALIST

This is a font styling program capable of transforming fonts into display type. The program has 120 unique special effects that work with any font in a system, and it can output to virtually any device. There is full color support, import/export capabilities, and compatibility with painting and drawing programs, desktop publishing, and word processing programs.

System requirements: Macintosh Plus or later, 1 MB of RAM. *Suggested retail price*: $179.95.

Postcraft International, Inc., 27811 Hopkins Ave., Suite 6, Valencia, CA 91355. Phone: 805-257-1797, fax: 805-257-1759.

INFINI-D

An animation package that creates photorealistic images and animation. Anything can be animated with the unique visual animation sequencer

including lights, objects, surfaces, and cameras. It completely integrates modeling, rendering, and animation.

System requirements: Macintosh II family, 4 MB of RAM, 8- or 24- bit color, System 6.0.5 or later. *Suggested retail price*: $895.

Specular International, Box 888, Amherst, MA 01004. Phone: 413-549-7600; fax: 413-549-15631.

KAI'S POWER TOOLS

A filter plug-in for Painter, Photoshop, and others. It has real-time previews, channel operation apply nodes, and preset viewing; works with 500 colors at one time.

System requirements: Macintosh System 7, at least 4 MB of RAM and 4 MB hard drive, color display. *Suggested retail price*: $199.

HSC Software, 1661 Lincoln Blvd., Suite 101, Santa Monica, CA 90404. Phone: 310-392-8441, fax: 310-392-6015.

KPT BRYCE

A 3-D rendering program. You can use preset skies and terrains or create your own. It has a module to create custom screen savers. Comes with controls

197

that let you manipulate surface contours, translucency, reflectivity, color, and alpha channels.

System requirements: Macintosh System 7, at least 4 MB of RAM and 4 MB hard drive, color display. *Suggested retail price*: $199.

HSC Software, 1661 Lincoln Blvd., Suite 101, Santa Monica, CA 90404. Phone: 310-392-8441, fax: 310-392-6015.

MORPH

This program smoothly transforms one image into another (*morphing*). Graphics can be generated from Macintosh-compatible painting and drawing programs, and digitized or scanned images.

System requirements: Macintosh LC or later, System 6.0 or later. *Suggested retail price*: $149.

Gryphon Software Corp., 7220 Trade St., Suite 120, San Diego, CA 92121. Phone: 619-536-8815; fax: 619-536-8932.

PIXAR TYPESTRY (PIXAR)

This software turns TrueType and Type 1 fonts into three-dimensional images. Fonts are converted into objects that can be rotated, scaled uniformly or nonuniformly, extruded, blurred, patterned, shadowed, and embossed, among other special effects.

System requirements: Macintosh II, 8 MB of RAM, math coprocessor, 32-bit QuickDraw, Multifinder, System 6.0.5 or later.

Pixar, 1001 W. Cutting Blvd., Richmond, CA 94804. Phone: 510-236-4000; fax 510-236-0388.

RAY DREAM DESIGNER

This is a three-dimensional modeling and rendering application that produces full color photorealistic 3-D artwork. This program is capable of handling the complexities of 3-D. It automatically creates lighting, shadows, transparency, reflections, and perspective.

System requirements: Any color-capable Macintosh with a math coprocessor, 5 MB of RAM, a hard drive, 8- or 24-bit video board recommended, 32-bit QuickDraw 1.2 or later, and System 6.0.5 or later. *Suggested retail price*: $299.

Ray Dream, Inc., 1804 N. Shoreline Blvd., Mountain View, CA 94043. Phone: 415-960-0765, fax: 415-960-1198.

SHOWPLACE

Users can create realistic, high-impact, three-dimensional graphics with this program. Objects can be viewed from different angles, arranged in different scenes, and set lights, all without learning complex rendering and modeling technologies.

Suggested retail price: $695.

Pixar, 1001 W. Cutting Blvd., Richmond, CA 94804. Phone: 510-236-4000; fax: 510-236-0388.

STRATA STUDIO PRO

A professional sophisticated application that creates 3-D illustrations and animation. It has tools for rendering and animation and can be used with QuickTime to create movies.

Suggested retail price: $949.

Strata Inc., Two W. Saint George Blvd., Suite 2100, St. George, UT 84770. Phone: 800-628-5218; fax: 801-628-9756.

STRATA VISION 3D

This is a computer illustration program that creates photorealistic, three-dimensional modeling, scene composition, rendering, and animation. There are unlimited light sources of varying types. Transparency, refraction, shad-

ows, transparent shadows, image mapping, texture mapping, and smooth shading are just a few of the rendering options available. This program is also compatible with QuickTime technology.

System requirements: Macintosh II family or LC with Floating Point Unit (FPU), 4 MB of RAM, hard disk, 32-bit color QuickDraw, System 6.0.3 or later.

Strata Inc., Two W. Saint George Blvd., Suite 2100, St. George, UT 84770. Phone: 800-628-5218; fax: 801-628-9756.

COLOR EDITING AND PROCESSING

ADOBE PHOTOSHOP

This is a photo design and production tool that allows creation of original images using advanced painting functions. It features a wide selection of painting and editing tools, custom tools and brushes, special effects, textures, and patterns. A number of image types are supported including grayscale, RGB, HSL, and CMYK. There is tremendous control over display colors.

System requirements: Macintosh SE or larger, including portables. *Suggested retail price*: $895.

Adobe Systems, Inc., 1585 Charleston Rd., Mountain View, CA 94039. Phone: 415-961-4400 or 800-833-6687.

ALDUS DIGITAL DARKROOM

This is an image processing program that works like a darkroom to enhance and compose scanned images, such as photos. Some of the features included are automatic image manipulation, detailed retouching, AutoTrace, unique selection tools, and image enhancement.

System requirements: Macintosh Plus or larger, 1 MB of RAM, hard disk drive recommended, System 6.0.4 or later. *Suggested retail price*: $395.

Aldus Corp., 9770 Carrol Center Rd., San Diego, CA 92126. Phone; 619-695-6956, fax: 619-695-7902.

CIS COLORACCESS

This is color separation software that imitates the capabilities of drum scanners. Users can achieve high-quality color reproduction, tonal compression, color accuracy, and sharpening. ColorAccess works with any image saved in a Photoshop file format, which means it can be used with desktop scanners.

System requirements: Macintosh II, 5 MB of RAM, hard disk drive, System 6.0.5 or later, CIS 3515 or CIS 4520 RS recommended.

PixelCraft, A Xerox Co., 130 Doolittle Dr., San Leonardo, CA 94577. Phone: 510-562-2480, fax: 510-562-6451.

KODAK COLORSENSE COLOR MANAGER

This program simplifies color balance for the entire system. The colors seen on the monitor will match the colors on the original scanned photographs, transparencies, or Photo CD as well as the output from a printer. Included is a hardware tool that calibrates the monitor for consistent screen display over time and a scanner target for scanner calibration.

Suggested retail price: $499.

Eastman Kodak Co., Digital Pictorial Hard Copy & Printer Products Division, 343 State St., Rochester, NY 14650. Phone: 800-242-2424 or 800-465-6523 in Canada.

POSTERWORKS

This program can generate point-of-purchase displays, posters, tradeshow exhibits, theatrical backdrops, and billboards. There are many unique controls including tools to configure layout size, vary panel size, gap between panels, overlay, and printer calibration. A complete library of pre-designed templates is included.

System requirements: Macintosh II or larger, 2 MB of RAM, 20 MB hard disk drive, System 6.0.3 or later.

S. H. Pierce & Co., One Kendall Square, Suite 323, Building 600, Cambridge, MA 02139. Phone: 617-338-2222, fax: 617-338-2223.

BACKGROUNDS AND TEXTURES

ATMOSPHERES BACKGROUND SYSTEMS

This program provides full-page color and grayscale background images, plus Watermark—a special-effects software tool. Watermark allows the user to change image color intensity (*ghosting*) to permit text placement over the background artwork. Backgrounds are high resolution to provide output of professional quality on laser printers, imagesetters, four-color printing, 35mm transparencies, and on-screen.

System requirements: Macintosh Plus or larger, hard disk drive with 1 MB free, SuperDrive, System 6.0.7 or later. *Suggested retail price*: $129.

TechPool Studios, 1463 Warrensville Center Rd., Cleveland, OH 44121. Phone: 800-777-8930, fax: 216-382-1915.

FOLIO 1 PRINT PRO CD

This is a collection of 100 photographic backgrounds and textures for graphic design. They are categorized under the headings of Abstract, Fabric, Food, Marble, Masonry, Metal, Nature, Novelties, Paper, and Wood. There is unlimited editing.

System requirements: Macintosh SE/30, LC, II, or Quadra; CD-ROM drive. *Suggested retail price*: $499.95.

D'pix, Inc., 414 W. Fourth Ave., Columbus, OH 43201. Phone: 800-238-3749, fax: 619-294-0002.

FOUNTAIN VIEW

This is an assemblage of 104 gradient screens (*fountains*) and a utility program that allows the suer to create new fountains. Each fountain may be viewed in relation to other page elements, then positioned, sized, and selected to change its shape. A fountain modifier is included, allowing users to create new fountains of any halftone and screen angle.

System requirements: Macintosh Plus or larger. *Suggested retail price*: $75.

Isis Imaging Corp., 3400 Inverness St., Vancouver, BC, Canada V5V 4V5. Phone: 604-873-8878.

IMAGECELS CD-ROM

This is a library collection of 1,150 royalty-free photorealistic high-resolution texture maps, full screen backgrounds, and images. Included are 14 common file formats.

System requirements: Macintosh II, 2 MB of RAM, hard disk drive, CD-ROM drive. *Suggested retail price*: $495.

IMAGETECTS, 7200 Bollinger Rd., San Jose, CA 95129. Phone: 408-252-5487, fax: 408-252-7409.

PIXAR 128

This program creates graphic visual effects that can be integrated with any 128 TiFF formatted digital texture in design, video, and multimedia applications. There is a library of unique high-quality textures that can be tiled for high-resolution images.

Suggested retail price: $198.

Pixar, 1001 W. Cutting Blvd., Richmond, CA 94804. Phone: 510-236-4000; fax 510-236-0388.

POWER BACKGROUNDS

This program features high-tech PICT file sin 35mm color slide backgrounds. A manual is included with psychological effects of color and complete indexes and illustrations of design and color combinations.

System requirements: Macintosh Plus or larger. *Suggested retail price*: $97.50.

California Clip Art, 1750 California St., Corona, CA 92719. Phone: 909-272-1474, fax: 909-272-3979.

STRATASHAPES

This is a collection of three-dimensional objects for creating photorealistic images and animation in StrataVision. The library is comprised of predefined 3-D geometry and real-life material attributes. Some of the library shapes are Lighting, Furniture, and Starter.

System requirements: Macintosh II family or LC with floating point unit (FPU), hard disk drive, StrataVision 3d. *Suggested retail price*: $179.

Strata Inc., Two W. Saint George Blvd., Suite 2100, St. George, UT 84770. Phone: 800-628-5218, fax: 801-628-9756.

STRATATEXTURES

This is an assemblage of surface and solid textures in libraries that allow the user to apply predefined attributes to three-dimensional objects. The libraries include wood textures, stone textures, metal textures, tile textures, brick textures, off-beat textures, solid textures, and starter textures. These libraries impart greater flexibility when creating photorealistic illustrations by increasing the available surface options.

System requirements: Macintosh II family or LC with floating point unit (FPU), hard disk drive, StrataVision 3d. *Suggested retail price*: $139.

Strata Inc., Two W. Saint George Blvd., Suite 2100, St. George, UT 84770. Phone: 800-628-5218, fax: 801-628-9756.

VISUALS

This extension consists of specialized libraries that contain wallpaper, stone, interior, still life, and flooring. The visuals are created with seamless edges. This allows for perfect mapping in three-dimensional render programs and three-dimensional text programs. Included is a manual with individual specs on each texture and hints on how to apply them.

System requirements: Macintosh II or larger. *Suggested retail price*: $50 to $70.

Visual Imagineers, 748 North Highway 67, Florissant, MO 63031. Phone: 314-838-2653.

WRAPTURES 1 AND 2

These are CD-ROM libraries of seamless tileable textures. Wraptures 1 includes a wide rang of image categories, such as architecture, astronomy, earth and moon, botanical, natural elements, gumbo, and others. A utility called Browser is included on the disk; it allows the user to scan the textures and copy them to the hard drive.

System requirements: Macintosh LC or larger, CD-ROM drive. *Suggested retail price*: $129.

Form and Function, Dist. by Educorp, 7434 Trade St., San Diego, Ca 92121. Phone: 800-843-9497, fax: 619-536-2345.

IMAGING UTILITIES

ALDUS FETCH

This is a multiuser, mixed-media database that allows users to catalog, browse, and retrieve images, animations, and sound files. Without open-

203

ing the source application, each image and movie can be viewed, and the sound files can be heard. All file formats are supported and can be stored and retrieved from anywhere on a network.

System requirements: Macintosh Classic, SE/30, or larger; 4 MB of RAM, (5 MB recommended); hard disk drive; System 6.0.7 or later. *Suggested retail price*: $295.

Aldus Corp., 411 First Ave. South, Suite 200, Seattle, WA 98104. Phone: 206-622-5500.

DEBABELIZER

This program can be used by anyone who creates or uses graphics, by providing automated graphics processing and translation. It is a complement to paint, drawing, or image-editing software. A set of functions enhances the ability to process graphics. When used with its internal scripting function, graphics are automatically edited, manipulated, and translated.

System requirements: Macintosh Plus or larger, hard disk drive, System 6.0.7 or later. *Suggested retail price*: $299.

Equilibrium. 475 Gate Five Rd., Sausalito, CA 94965. Phone: 800-524-8651, fax: 415-332-4433.

ENHANCE

This is an image analysis and enhancement application with a combination of sophisticated paint, filter, and retouching tools that manipulate grayscale images. Users can open and edit multiple files larger than available memory. To protect against unwanted mistakes and for greater flexibility, multiple undos are available. High-speed image filters to improve brightness and contrast levels and enhanced image features that perform special effects are provided.

System requirements: Macintosh SE/30 or larger, 2 MB of RAM, hard disk drive, System 6.0.5 or later, 32-bit color QuickDraw. *Suggested retail price*: $375.

MicroFrontier, Inc., 3401 101st St., Suite E, Des Moines, IA 50322. Phone: 515-270-8109, fax: 515-278-6828.

FASTEDDIE

This program compresses and converts 24-bit images without the loss of image quality. Bitmapped and low-resolution grayscale images can be converted to high-quality grayscale images through proprietary sampling routines. The converted files can be imported into page layout or manipulation applications that read and write standard file formats.

System requirements: Macintosh II or Quadra, 4 MB of RAM, hard disk drive, color monitor, System 6.0.5 or later. *Suggested retail price*: $169.

LizardTech, Box 2129, Santa Fe, NM 87504. Phone: 505-989-7117, fax: 505-989-9292.

IMPRESSIT

This program provides compression and decompression of grayscale images. Image preview window, thumbnail, snapshot, virtual memory, and Adobe Photoshop plug-ins are all included. If automatic image compression is selected, images are compressed when they are saved to the hard disk. The compression process is transparent to the user when this is executed.

System requirements: Macintosh II family. *Suggested retail price*: $159.

Radius Inc., 1710 Fortune Dr., San Jose, CA 95131. Phone: 800-227-2795, fax: 408-434-6437.

JAG II

This program is used for resolution boosting and to eliminate the jaggies (stair-stepped edges) on digital images and animation. Performs on paint images, scans, animation, 3-D illustrations, multimedia, and bit-mapped images. Most Macintosh file formats are supported.

System requirements: Macintosh color capable, 2 MB of RAM, hard disk drive, 8- or 24-bit video board recommended, System 6.0.5 or later. *Suggested retail price*: $115.

Ray Dream Inc., 1804 N. Shoreline Blvd., Mountain View, CA 94043. Phone: 415-960-0765, fax: 415-960-1198.

KODAK COLORSQUEEZE

This is image-compression software. PICT an 24-bit TIFF files can be compressed and reconstructed to their original size when needed. Thumbnails of compressed files can be viewed quickly on the monitor. There is a preview option that allows the user to see a series of images before selecting one to uncompress.

System requirements: Macintosh II family, System 6.0.3 or later. *Suggested retail price*: $179.

Eastman Kodak Co., Personal Printer Products, 343 State St., Rochester, NY 14650. Phone: 800-242-2424 or 800-465-6523 in Canada.

MULTI-AD SEARCH

This is an image cataloging and retrieval system. Users can open or search multiple catalogs and print text lists or catalogs. Many Macintosh file formats are supported.

System requirements: Macintosh Plus or larger, 2 MB of RAM, System 6.0.3 or later. *Suggested retail price*: $249.

Multi-Ad Services, Inc., 1720 W. Detweiller Dr., Peoria, IL 61615. Phone: 309-692-1530.

OFOTO

This is scanning software that scans photographs and line art. Autoscan straightens, crops, eliminates moire patterns, and ensures precision line art. Adaptive Calibration matches the scanned image to the original image, automatically.

System requirements: Macintosh Plus or larger, 1 MB of RAM, hard disk drive, System 6.0.7 or later. *Suggested retail price*: $395.

Light Source, Inc., 17 E. Sir Francis Drake Blvd., Larkspur, CA 94939. Phone: 415-461-8000, fax: 415-461-8011.

Command
Key Shortcuts

APPENDIX B

CANVAS MENU

Dry (wet layer)	**Command-Y**
Grid	**Command-G**
Resize image	**Shift-Command-R**
Tracing paper	**Command-T**

CLONING

Relink clone source	**Option-Clone Command**
Set clone source	**Brush-Option**

COLOR SETS

Add current color to set	**Shift-Command-K**
Replace current color in set	**Option**

DROPPER

Measure mask density	**Shift**

EDIT MENU

Copy	**Command-C**
Cut	**Command-X**
Deselect	**Command-D**
Drop current floater	**Shift-Command-D**
Paste	**Command-V**
Reselect	**Command-R**
Select all	**Command-A**
Undo	**Command-Z**

EFFECTS MENU

Adjust colors	**Shift-Command-A**
Equalize	**Command-E**
Fill	**Command-F**
Last effect	**Command-/**
Second-to-last effect	**Command-;**

FILE MENU

Close	**Command-W**
Get info	**Command-I**
New	**Command-N**
Open	**Command-O**
Print	**Command-P**
Quit	**Command-Q**
Save	**Command-S**

FLOATER LIST

Adjust opacity in 10% increments	**1 to 0 keys**
Attribute dialog for current floater	**Enter**
Item layer order	**Click-and-drag item in list**
Select/deselect list items	**Shift**

FLOATING SELECTION TOOL

Attribute dialog for current floater	**Enter**
Delete selected floaters	**Delete**
Duplicate	**Option-click**
Hide/display marquee	**Shift-Command-H**
Move floater by 1 screen pixel	**Arrow keys**

FRAME STACK NAVIGATION

First frame of stack	**Home**
Last frame of stack	**End**
Next frame	**Page up**
Previous frame	**Page down**
Stop at current frame	**Stop button-Option**
Top and return to start	**Command-.**

MAGIC WAND

Add color to selection	**Shift-Wand**
Find all instances in area	**Selection rectangle**

OUTLINE SELECTION TOOL—BEZIÉR

Corner/curve toggle	**Control-drag on handle**
Delete last point	**Delete**
Equal length handles	**Shift-drag on handle**
Make last point corner	**Option-drag on point**

OUTLINE SELECTION TOOL—FREEHAND

Add area	**Command**
Close path	**Enter**
Edit path	**Shift**
Stroke width change with pressure	**Control**
Subtract area	**Command-Option**

OUTLINE SELECTION TOOL—STRAIGHT LINE

Close path	**Enter**
Constrain at 45° angles	**Shift**

OVAL SELECTION TOOL

Constrain to circle	**Control**

PAINT BUCKET

Limit fill extent	**Click-and-drag paint bucket**
Magic wand fill	**Command-Click-and-drag paint bucket**

PAINTING BRUSH CONTROLS

Adjust opacity in 10% increments	**1 to 0 keys**
Build brush	**Command-B**
Constrain (straight-line mode)	**Shift**
Resize brush	**Command-Option**

PALETTES

Advanced controls	**Command-7**
Art materials	**Command-3**
Brush controls	**Command-4**
Brushes	**Command-2**
Color sets	**Command-8**
Controls	**Command-6**
Objects	**Command-5**
Tools	**Command-1**

PATH ADJUSTER TOOL

Delete selected paths	**Delete**
Duplicate	**Option-click**
Move path by 1 screen pixel	**Arrow keys**
Render/unrender path	**Enter**

PATH ADJUSTER—DYNAMIC

Resize	**Corner handles**
Resize/one dimension	**Side handles**
Resize/preserve aspect	**Shift-corner handles**
Rotate	**Command-corner handles**
Skew	**Command-side handles**

PATH LIST

Attribute dialog for selected path	**Double-click**
Item layer order	**Click-and-drag item in list**
Render/unrender path	**Enter**
Select/deselect list items	**Shift**

RECTANGULAR SELECTION TOOL

Adjust current selection rectangle	**Shift**
Constrain to square	**Control**
Edit selection dialog	**Shift-Command-E**

SCREEN NAVIGATION

Center image	**Spacebar-click**
Constrain rotate to 90°	**Shift-Option-Spacebar**
Define magnification area	**Click-and-drag**
Rotate image	**Spacebar-Option**
Scroll image with grabber	**Spacebar**
Unrotate image	**Spacebar-Option-click**
Zoom in	**Spacebar-Command**
Zoom out	**Spacebar-Command-Option**

SPIRAL GRADATIONS

Adjust spirality	**Command-angle adjuster**

TOOLS MENU

Build brush	**Command-B**
Edit rectangular selection	**Command-Shift-E**
Load nozzle	**Command-L**

WET LAYER

Post-diffuse	**Shift-D**

WINDOWS MENU

Full screen window	**Command-M**
Hide/display palettes	**Command-H**
Zoom in	**Command-+**
Zoom out	**Command--**

Add-on
Libraries

APPENDIX C

Fractal Design Corporation has available at a nominal cost add-on textures and brush looks libraries. These libraries expand the functionality of Painter and make things much more interesting. This appendix gives you a quick preview of what's available.

REALLY COOL TEXTURES VOLUME 1: GRAINS AND WEAVES

GRAINS LIBRARY

 Rough Water

 Basic Paper

 Big Canvas

 Raw Canvas

 Fine Grain

 Complex Canvas

 Angular Grain

 Rosette

 Rough

 Felt

WEAVES LIBRARY

 Omniwicker

 Fleece

 Strokes

 Wove

 Wicked Weave

 Bristles

 Basket 1

 Basket 2

 Small Weave

 Fiberfill

REALLY COOL TEXTURES VOLUME 2: PATTERNS AND NATURE

PATTERNS LIBRARY

 Tigerskin

 Acid Etch

 Squeal

 Formless

 Thumb Print

 Sun Surface

 Intermezzo

 Knobs

 Nubs

 Puzzle

NATURE LIBRARY

 Rock

 Coral

 Big Crackle

 Small Crackle

 Clouds

 Mountains

 Taffy

 Swirly

 Painted Wave

 Etched

BRUSH LOOKS VOLUME 1: TREES AND LEAVES

TREES LIBRARY

 Ivy

 Sprouts

Ferns

215

Twigs

 Eucalyptus

 Sprigs

 Daisies

 Leaves

 Vines

 Umbrella Plant

 Grass

 Branches

 Maple Leaves

 Brambles

 Thorns

 Hanging Moss

 Bare Trees

 Douglas Fir

 Ground Cover

LEAVES LIBRARY

 Mimosa

 Thick Grass

 Pine Needles

 Sassafras

 Seedlings

To order any of these libraries, contact Fractal Design Corporation at 355 Spreckels Drive, Aptos, CA 95003, (408) 688-5300. Individual libraries are $29.95, or get all three for $59.95, plus shipping.

Notes on Upgrading

APPENDIX D

NOTES ON UPGRADING FROM PAINTER 2.X

Upgrading from version 2.x is a breeze! Simply follow the regular installation instructions given in Chapter 1. Your upgrade contains a new serial number, which you should use from now on. Your old serial number won't work and won't be accepted for upgrades.

LIBRARIES

The installation places all Painter 3 files in a Painter 3 folder. Most version 2.x owners have their old version in a Painter 2.x folder. If you have any libraries for version 2.x, simply copy them from your Painter 2.x folder to the new Painter 3 folder. When you are ready to use them, use the **Library** buttons in the appropriate drawer. Everything is fully upward compatible from version 2.x, but not from version 1.x.

If you have any add-on libraries, such as those in Appendix C, you can move them from your Painter 2.x folder into the Painter 3 folder. If it seems easier to you, you may also simply reinstall them into the Painter 3 folder.

COLOR PAGES

Version 2.x color pages can be turned into version 3.0 color sets. Launch Painter 3, press **Esc**, then **Shift+K**. Select the Painter 2.x settings file from the dialog box, press **OK**, and a Painter 3 color set is generated for each Painter 2.x color page.

CUSTOM BRUSH SETS

If you created any custom brushes in Painter 2.x, use Painter 2.x's **Brush Mover** to create a library of the brushes you want to port into Painter 3. Copy the library into your Painter 3 folder, then open Painter 3 and use the **Brush Mover** to load them.

VERSION 2.X FILES

Version 2.x RIFF-format files are fully upward compatible with version 3. In fact, version 3 files are downward-compatible with version 2.x (except for those with a mask layer).

FREE UP SOME DISK SPACE

When you are sure you have all of your customized items removed from your Painter 2.x folder, you may delete it.

Glossary

alpha channel A 32-bit color system used to mask areas for transparencies, overlays, and special effects.

bitmap A graphic image represented by individual dots (pixels) laid out on a grid.

camera-ready copy Graphics, illustration, text, etc. in its final form ready to be photographed for reproduction.

chromalin Translucent color photographic film, sometimes called a *transparency* or a *chrome*.

clone An exact copy of an image. When using a cloned image, the source document must remain on screen.

CMYK color A color model using cyan (C), magenta (M), yellow (Y), and black (K) as the basic inks to form different colors. It is generally used for color separations.

color key A method developed by the 3M Company that shows progressive color breakdown. The resulting proofs are useful for checking registration, size, and blemishes. Color keys are not a good method for checking actual color.

comp Abbreviation for composition layout. A mock-up of a design to be used by the client or designer.

concentration Intensity and saturation of paint.

continuous tone An unscreened photograph or illustration containing gradient tones from black to white.

curved path Used to draw Beziér curves. They are solid outlines with points and handles. You can import and export curve paths.

cyan A greenish-blue color used in process color printing.

desktop publishing Using computers to produce high-quality text and graphics output to be sent to commercial printers. The common abbreviation is DTP.

dot gain A defect in printing when temperature, ink, and paper type cause an increase in the size of each drop of ink.

double-burning A process by which two images are imposed on each other for the purpose of creating one image.

DPI (*dots per inch*) A printer resolution measurement.

dye transfer A continuous-tone print produced from a transparency.

dye-sublimation print A color printing method that uses dye, instead of ink, to produce continuous color that approaches photographic quality.

EPS (*encapsulated PostScript*) A high-resolution graphic format that allows you to manipulate and preview your image on screen.

feathering Blending the edges of an object in an irregular way.

floaters Independent background images, which create complex compositions.

FPO Placing of art work "for position only" and not for reproducing.

frame stack A set of images that Painter tools individually manipulates. They can be played back as an animation, exported to QuickTime files, or have batch operation applied to them.

halftone A continuous image made by a screen that causes the image to be broken into various sized dots. Smaller dots produce lighter areas, and larger dots produce darker areas.

HSV (*hue, saturation, and value*) A color model that relates to the way the human eye perceives color. Painter uses HSV as the model for its color palette because this color-wheel-based system is most familiar to artists.

hue The property of a particular color relating to its frequency, or wavelength of light.

image hose A unique tool that paints with pictures instead of paint. Images are used with each brush stroke. These can be created textures or tiled patterns.

ink-jet printing As paper moves through the printer, rows of minute jets squirt ink to form an image.

LPI (*lines per inch*) A resolution measurement for halftone screens.

luminance The amount of light radiated by a monitor.

magenta A bluish-red color used in process color printing.

mask representation path Shown as a green and white dashed line. used the same way selections are used. When you paint, import, or generate masks from color or image, Painter calculates representative paths for the created data.

masking Blocking out part of an image to deselect it, to get rid of unwanted details, or to add to it.

mechanical Camera-ready art that has been physically put together by cut-and-paste methods.

multimedia Information from several sources using graphics, text, audio, and full-motion video.

outline path A selection not rendered into a mask. It shows up as a red or black line.

pen tablet A graphics drawing tablet used for sketching, drawing, and painting in conjunction with drawing or painting software.

penetration The degree to which paint permeates into paper.

pixel Short for picture element. The smallest element or dot that can be seen on a computer screen.

plates The actual thin sheet of metal or plastic on a printing press containing the image to be printed. When it is inked, it produces the printed master.

PMS (*Pantone Matching System*) A worldwide system of standardized ink colors used to specify and check color.

PostScript A computer language used to describe images and type for laser printers and other output devices developed and trademarked by Adobe Systems, Inc.

prepress The complete preparation of camera-ready materials up to printing.

process color Also called *four-color process*. Mixing the four standard printing color inks (see CMYK) to create images. A transparency is made for each individual color, and the color effect is created by overlapping the four transparent ink colors.

QuickTime A multiplatform extension to Macintosh system software. The video and animation data are turned into a frame stack. Exporting a Painter frame stack to QuickTime embellishes and synchronizes sound with other effects in video-editing applications.

RAM (*random access memory*) The amount of space your computer provides to temporarily store information. RAM space is considered volatile, as anything stored in it is erased when your computer is turned off.

resample Changing the resolution of an image.

RGB color Typically used to create transmitted colors, and the method used by color monitors and color televisions. RGB shows colors by using clusters of red, green, and blue phosphors, often referred to as *pixels*.

RIP (*raster image processor*) Prepares data for an output device, usually a printer.

saturation The extent to which a color is comprised of a selected hue, rather than a combination of hue and white, as in the difference between red (a heavily saturated color) and pink (a less saturated color).

scanning Converting line art, photographs, text, or graphics from paper to a bitmapped image for manipulation and placement on a computer.

spot color Color applied only to a specific area. At the time of color separation, the spot color is assigned its own plate.

stripping The physical placement of photographs, illustrations, text, graphics, and color areas in preparation to making a plate.

stylus A pressure-sensitive pen-like instrument that enables you to control the rate of flow from a tool in a drawing or painting program.

targa file A file format most common in higher-end PC-based paint systems.

thermal wax printing A medium-resolution printing process that transfers paraffin-based pigments onto paper.

TIFF (*tagged image file format*) A versatile graphics format, developed by Aldus Corp. and Microsoft Corp., that stores a map that specifies the location and color of each pixel.

transparency Color translucent photographic film, sometimes called a *chrome* or *chromalin*.

trapping An overlapping technique that allows for misregistration of the color plate to prevent gaps in color.

value The degree of lightness or darkness in a color.

Index

FRACTAL DESIGN PAINTER

227

INSTALLING THE PAINTER DEMO

The CD ROM included with *Fractal Design Painter* 3 *for the Macintosh* contains demonstration software for Fractal Design 3, several images, plus information on Fractal Design. Start the Painter Demo by double-clicking on Painter DEMO Installer INTL. Please note that this demo version of Painter does not print or save your files, nor will it record a session.

Please refer to the contents of this book for instructions on how to create a new document, open existing documents, and how to use Painter's vast palette of features. Use the Painter Demo and the step-by-step practice sessions offered in the book to get the most out of your introduction to Painter.

For all the images included on this disk, all rights are reserved by individual artists. Any reproduction is strictly prohibited unless prior, expressed written consent is obtained from the artist.

For more information on Fractal Design products call Fractal Design Corporation at 1-800-297-COOL.

To Purchase limited edition Fiery prints or archival quality Iris prints (on high-quality substrates) of any of the artwork printed in this book, or to find out about additional artwork by any of the artists featured in this book, please contact the authors at:

2542 NORTH FOURTH STREET, BOX 324
FLAGSTAFF, AZ 86004
(602) 526-6469

VISA and MASTERCARD accepted.